"*The Retirement Boom* is one of those just-in-time thought-provoking tools that gives you practical checklists, best-life strategies, and a healthy dose of caution and encouragement. It is a great read for anyone who's ready to take control of creating a personal plan for retirement. It also serves as a gentle, but effective nudge for anyone who has delayed taking steps to prepare for this critical phase of life."

—Sharon C. Taylor, senior vice president,
Human Resources, Prudential

"Finally! The definitive book on creating a purposeful and fulfilling second half of life. Inspiring and practical, filled with real-life stories and good sense, this book will give its readers the know-how to clarify their dreams and realize their true potential. It is a road map to a joyful encore life that is uniquely one's own, formed by experience and wisdom and self-awareness. A life changer!"

—Linda Watt, former U.S. Ambassador to Panama; former CEO, The Episcopal Church; Encore Innovation Fellow, 2013–2014

"*The Retirement Boom* offers a powerful perspective on how to make the golden years also be the renaissance period of your life. A compelling read to enrich and live life to its fullest and take advantage of all its bounty while not squandering the so-called retirement years."

—Rakesh Gangwal co-founder, IndiGo; former chairman, president and CEO, Worldspan Technologies, Inc.;
former president and CEO, U.S. Airways Group

"These authors have nailed it. Say good-bye retirement and hello to the best years of your life. *The Retirement Boom* provides the tools you need to redefine your 'golden years,' turning them into exactly what you had in mind, regardless of what that vision is."

—Susan C. Keating, president and CEO, National Foundation for Credit Counseling

"*The Retirement Boom* is a must read for anyone who wants to have a rewarding, meaningful and financially secure life post retirement. It is also a wake-up call for Boomers, particularly women, who have not adequately planned for the savings they will need as well as for policymakers and corporate human

resource officials to more creatively address financial planning for those who will be leaving the formal workforce. This book is timely, practical and compelling."

—Melanne Verveer, former U.S. Ambassador for Global Women's Issues, U.S. Department of State

"Reading *The Retirement Boom* is like meeting up with a trusted friend who is a combination of career mentor, financial advisor, innovative thinker, and "idea" person about the process of retirement—a process that clearly deserves serious rethinking! It opens up new vistas of opportunity, with practical suggestions for anyone contemplating a transition in their life and work. The authors meet a great need for the Baby Boomer and older population with an exciting, refreshing analysis of the "retirement" process. This book will be read widely and discussed deeply! Bring on the revolution!"

—Dr. Brady Deaton, former Chancellor, University of Missouri

"As Americans live longer lives, it is increasingly important for both our health and our wealth that we find fulfilling ways to remain engaged in society and our economy. This book provides a 'how-to' guide for individuals making this transition. Here's hoping that our public policies also pivot to helping Americans realize retirement as a period of productive change rather than withdrawal."

—Charles Blahous, Research Fellow, The Hoover Institution

"*The Retirement Boom* is a hands-on practical guide to plan for our next life stage after a traditional career. I am retiring this year, and rather than putting a period on my life, retirement is going to be filled with exclamation marks!!! It is never too late to "reboot" and "reinvent." After reading this book you will be ready to move into another chapter of your life. Read this book. It will excite your future and help you turn SUCCESS INTO SIGNIFICANCE!!!!"

—Joan Cronan, Women's Athletics Director Emeritus, University of Tennessee

An All-Inclusive Guide
to Money, Life, and Health
in Your Next Chapter

The
RETIREMENT
BOOM

By

CATHERINE ALLEN, NANCY BEARG,
RITA FOLEY, AND JAYE SMITH

FOREWORD BY ALAN WEBBER

CAREER
PRESS

THE CAREER PRESS, INC.
Wayne, NJ

THE RETIREMENT BOOM

EDITED BY JODI BRANDON
TYPESET BY EILEEN MUNSON

Cover design by Rob Johnson
Printed in the U.S.A.

To order this title, please call toll-free 1-800-CAREER-1 (NJ and Canada: 201-848-0310) to order using VISA or MasterCard, or for further information on books from Career Press.

The Career Press, Inc.
12 Parish Drive
Wayne, NJ 07470
www.careerpress.com

Library of Congress Cataloging-in-Publication Data

Allen, Catherine (Writer on retirement)
  The retirement boom : an all inclusive guide to money, life, and health in your next chapter / by Catherine Allen, Nancy Bearg, Rita Foley, and Jaye Smith ; foreword by Alan Webber.
     pages cm
Includes index.
   ISBN 978-1-63265-016-0 (paperback) — ISBN 978-1-63265-982-8 (ebook) 1. Baby boom generation—Retirement—United States. 2. Retirement—United States—Planning. 3. Finance, Personal—United States. I. Bearg, Nancy J. II. Foley, Rita. III. Title.

HQ1063.2.U6A435 2015

306.3'80973—dc23

2015028937

We dedicate this book to everyone
who is seeking to
create a great next chapter of life.

Acknowledgments

We wrote this story for you—yes, all of you Baby Boomers, the generation that has the courage to dream, to dare, and to live life to its fullest. Thanks also to our parents for putting up with us, especially in the revolutionary times of the '60s—the inspiration for a major theme of the book!

Throughout the process of writing this book, many individuals have taken time to help us out. We express gratitude to our retreat attendees and interviewees for sharing your personal experiences. We are inspired by your stories as you are about to enter retirement or have recently jumped into this new chapter. When requested, we changed names in the book.

We applaud the corporations with which we have worked that see the need to support their soon-to-be retirees—their best advocates—as they enter their next phase in life.

This book would not have been possible without the support, skills, and encouragement of Julie Kline, Julie Koch-Beinke, Molly Clarke, Rachel Patterson, Linda Cashdan, Fern Reiss, Jean Carbain, Robin Sherin, Emily Koch, Susan Keating, Frank Faeth, Beth Strutzel, Kim Duncan, Virginia Baden, and Hollis Rafkin-Sax. And a big thank you to our literary agent Marilyn Allen.

Thank you to our families and many friends, who root us on and give us so much support, inspiration, and love.

Contents

Foreword

What's next?

That's the single most powerful question of our time. It's the question at the heart of this important and useful book; it's the question this book sets out to help a whole generation of newly minted seniors answer for themselves.

And it's a question that very few retiring Baby Boomers ever expected they would have to deal with—which is why this book is so valuable. For the most part, an entire generation of Americans simply surged ahead, from life phase to life phase, transforming the national landscape along the way.

When they entered kindergarten, the Boomers triggered a national educational revolution—a whole new public school infrastructure had to be created.

When they reached high school, the Boomers spawned a music and pop culture revolution—a whole new sound and a whole new scene entered American life.

When they headed off to college, the Boomers made history with political and social revolutions—movements were born to take on racism, challenge sexism, and champion environmentalism.

And so it makes complete sense that after intervening decades of entering the workforce, establishing families, participating in community affairs, and acting as responsible adults, Boomers today have arrived at a whole new phase of life: a phase in which this transformative and transforming generation will change what it means to retire—a retirement revolution is happening now.

But here's the difference.

Reimagining and reinventing retirement will actually take preparation. A generation that has simply surged forward, using its size and scale, its energy, and its creativity to forge a new life path, now has to stop and think. It has to ask the *What's next?* question—and then find the resources and resourcefulness to generate a whole new set of answers.

In fact, answering the *What's next?* question is the mandatory life skill of the 21st century—not only for Boomers, but for every generation that is making the journey of its lifetime.

Because the simple fact is, the old answers simply do not fit the new realities.

We are living longer lives. We are living healthier lives. We are living fuller lives. We have more choices, more options, and more possibilities than any generation in history.

But we share one thing in common with every generation: We are not prepared for these new realities.

We are offered an open-ended question with the opportunity for each of us to answer it in our own way. There is no one-size-fits-all response to the *What's next?* question—which is a challenge, a gift, and a blessing! Each of us can reimagine and reinvent our own way forward to the rest and for the rest of our lives.

Each of us will have to do it in our own way. But what we share is the need to do the real work of coming up with our own answer to that question. We need to develop the approach and the skills that will enable each of us to find the way forward into this uncharted territory—to channel our curiosity, choice, and courage to make decisions that offer each of us a future that is filled with purpose, passion, and personal growth.

That's where this book comes in.

It offers each of us a workable way to find our own answer. It suggests pragmatic practices and systematic solutions that will help each of us build the skills we need for this new phase of life. It is both down-to-earth and future-focused—practical as well as aspirational, the hallmark characteristics of the Boomers as a generation.

This book fits the moment we're in. It is what we need, exactly when we need it.

My advice is to take advantage of the exercises, to take heart from the stories, and to take hold of the message. Read this book—then pass it along to someone you care about, someone who could also benefit from the practical wisdom in these pages.

We are in a time of change and opportunity, a time of personal reinvention and social revolution.

In other words, it's a great time for discovery, innovation, and self-imagination.

It's a great time to get to work!

Alan Webber

Co-Founder of *Fast Company Magazine* and Co-Author of
Life Reimagined: Discovering Your New Life Possibilities

Santa Fe, New Mexico

CHAPTER 1

The "R" Word: Reboot and Reinvent Rather Than Retire

Twenty years from now you will be more disappointed by the things you didn't do than by the ones you did do. So throw off the bowlines. Sail away from the safe harbor. Catch the trade winds in your sails. Explore. Dream. Discover.

—Mark Twain

The concept of retirement is evolving and changing. The 76 million U.S. Baby Boomers (born between 1946 and 1964) who have redefined each stage of life as they passed through it are redefining this one as well. They are not going to retire like their parents or grandparents. With longer life spans, better health, and myriad opportunities to play, work, volunteer, travel, and try new things, Baby Boomers are exploring the next chapter of life with enthusiasm and creativity.

This book is about just that—revolutionary retirement. The Retirement Boom.

Some people embrace the "R" word; others are uncomfortable with it; all are interested in how it will impact them. In this opening chapter, we give you some background on the concept of retirement and introduce our major themes for the book, among them, revolution, rebooting, and reinventing—all key ingredients in describing the new phenomenon that is sweeping the Baby Boomer generation. We also talk about the critical importance of planning plus many other challenges and joys of this next exciting chapter of your life.

We will define some terms—as we use them—to get started, then describe the rest of the book.

Retirement: The lifestyle you choose after leaving a full-time career. It may involve continuing to work or not.

Revolution: It's not really a revolution the way the Beatles sang it to us, but Baby Boomers are creating revolutionary retirement—individually and as a group. It's a major change in the way things are done.

Rebooting: Rebooting is refreshing, renewing life, and beginning to transition to a new phase.

Reinvention: Reinvention is figuring out how to do the things that make you feel relevant, inspired, and inspiring.

Revolutionary Retirement

Remember when you were younger and your grandparents retired, or at least you heard about it? It was probably an important event, marked by a farewell ceremony or party and many congratulations on the career well done and the earned relaxation ahead. The Gold Watch.

Then maybe your parents retired, and it was similar. A long time spent in a career or job. Time ahead for well-earned leisure. Time to spend with the grandkids, even to fly frequently across country to see them. Congratulations. The Golden Years.

Now, you may be contemplating the "R" word yourself. But...golf, gardening, and grandchildren? Some embrace it.

But, many say: Who, me? Retire? Maybe later, maybe part-time. There's still too much to do in life to settle into a totally leisurely routine.

With possibly 30 more years of living after leaving a full-time career, the future requires some serious contemplation. Take it easy for a while? Volunteer? Start down a new career path? It is a time of exploration and doing things a new way.

Maybe the apt phrase about retirement these days (besides revolutionary) is "looking for more." Ten thousand Baby Boomers turn 65 every day, and they are looking for more—more life, more adventure, more discovery, more relaxation, more balance. They yearn for continued meaning, purpose, and contribution. They still seek an edge and a role, *relevance and fulfillment.*

They also want to maintain *identity and self-esteem.* For all those years, they were known as a worker of some sort: lawyer, teacher, member of the military, businessperson, baker, scientist, banker, plumber, office worker, farmer, mechanic. Many want a title that signifies that they are still in the mix, such as volunteer, consultant, author, instructor, counselor, advisor, board member, coach.

"Being retired" for many sounds too much like "out of action." But hear this: Retirees are not done. They are still active and involved—or at least they want to be. Life fills the space and yearns to take more shape.

It's never too late to balance the beloved aspects of retirement like grandkids and travel with an additional purpose—a new kind of work based on discovered insights, old skills or new skills, revived dreams or new interests.

Here are some of the many successful retirement stories we have heard:

When Helena retired from the World Bank, she wrote on her Facebook page: "Feels good to start my new life." That was and is her attitude, as she has settled into a new, full life in New Mexico balanced among leisure, volunteer activities, and plenty of travel and time with her grown children and friends. She does not miss work.

Jack, a lifelong architect, designed his next chapter by going back to school at age 69 to gain a doctorate degree in architecture with a philosophical base so he could fulfill another dream: to teach. Now in his 80s, he is a full-time teaching professor at Montana State University School of Architecture.

Suzanne says, "My spouse, David, is a remarkable specimen of retirement. He was a molecular biologist one day and the next day a gardener-furniture maker-trail maintainer-beer maker-etc. He has never looked back! Me, I'm easing into it." Both Americans, they now live part-time in Mexico.

Craig retired early from his job as a Seattle high-school marine biology teacher, but continued to take students on field trips and do some consulting. Patty retired five years after Craig and continued her passion of nurturing MESA (the organization she created that encourages girls and minorities toward math, engineering, and science) through occasional consulting. They've moved into the new house they built and love their new time together and with their grandchildren.

Priscilla says she has used her retirement from the U.S. State Department to expand on her profession by carrying her skills into the nonprofit sector to do the work she really wants to do. "I couldn't do what I am doing today building programs overseas if I were still in the U.S. government, but I can only do what I am doing because I am using the skills acquired in my previous career. And I love this new phase as a consultant because I have time to do more than work."

Planning Is Key; Design Is the Goal

Planning is essential to overcoming worries, and to designing and achieving a successful (and you define successful) lifestyle in retirement. It is the reality check that takes into account your desires and resources and puts them together on a defined path.

This is design: thinking about and packaging your own brand of retirement, from rebooting to reinvention and from phase to phase as life evolves. **Chapter 2: Planning and Designing Your Reinvention** has advice and practical approaches.

Desires need to be considered first. That sounds a bit startling, as resources may be the constraining factor, but without knowing what you want to do and how you really want to live, you cannot know what resources you need. It may be less than you think. If you have not planned, you do not know. Some of the overarching questions about your desires are: How do you want to feel? What do you want to do? With whom do you want to spend your time? Where do you want to live?

We have an exercise at the end of this chapter on readiness to retire, and **Chapter 2: Planning and Designing Your Reinvention** covers these and other questions about your desires and whether you are ready for retirement. The rest of the book leads you further into answers and your planning.

Two More Words: Fear and Financial

We haven't yet mentioned two words that we expect are on your mind: *fear* and *financial*.

Fear

Let's start with fear. It's hard to admit, but easy to feel. If the next phase of your life—a very major one—is unexplored or unplanned, such as in a forced retirement, it is an unknown, and trepidation can well up. You may worry about the issues we discussed earlier: relevance, fulfillment, identity, and self-esteem. *Who am I after I leave my job?* Even people who have a clear idea of what their retirement might look like have those worries. They ask: *How will I feel without the fixed schedule, daily demands, hundreds of e-mails, being "on" 24/7? Will I be wanted and needed? Will I be relevant?*

Another fear is: *What will I do with my time? Will I be busy enough or bored? Will I be boring?*

The way to overcome fear, we all know, is to face it. In this case, a way to face it is to acknowledge and explore the feelings. The questionnaire introduced at the end of this chapter should be helpful in that quest, as would talking it through with family and friends.

Financial

The other "F" word is *financial,* to which we devote all of **Chapter 3: Making Your Money Last,** even though this is not a financial book. Perhaps you are surprised that we have barely mentioned income so far because it's the topic everyone talks about—well, at least, banks and the increasingly alarming news reports focusing on the plight of many retirees in the wake of the recent recession. The rest of us may bring it up occasionally with an advisor or friends, or try to ignore it, especially if we are in the tranche of Baby Boomers farther away from age 65. But, we all know that it is super important. Too few Americans have paid enough attention to saving for retirement, or can't live and save on their earnings, or their savings have been diminished by the rough economic times. A recent U.S. government study reports that 75 percent of Baby Boomers are not financially prepared for retirement. Surely this is a wakeup call, individually and as a nation.

Whatever your means, fear comes in here—fear of not having enough money for the long life we hope we will have, and fear that government-sponsored retirement and healthcare (Social Security and Medicare) will collapse or fall short. There is also fear of using up our savings on our parents or on our grown children still in the nest, and fear of galloping health and long-term care costs as we age. Will we need a nursing home or around-the-clock nursing care?

The reality is that retirement at age 62 or 65 can no longer be assumed, due to finances (and longer lives). Millions will want to, or have to, work longer to have enough money. That requires planning and knowing what you have and how long it can last. Retirement always has required financial planning, but now it is critically important. The world is an uncertain place, and it is important to be flexible and able to deal with that ambiguity. **Chapter 3: Making Your Money Last** addresses the main issues of financial planning and provides resources to find your own answers. We'll mention again that this is not a financial retirement book, but we do cover innovative and important information on financial planning that will be very helpful to you.

Starting a New Chapter of Work

Retirement need not be an abrupt work stop or be career-ending. It can be a gradual phasing out of the regular, full-time work that paid the bills and consumed your working life for decades. Or it could be a replacement type of work—a part-time gig using the knowledge and skills from your old job, a different line of work based on a revived or new interest, or volunteering. Indeed, many people in their 50s, 60s, 70s, and 80s are still working, starting new careers, exploring non-profit involvement, or launching their own businesses. **Chapter 4: Reinventing Into New Work** explores the ways Boomers are discovering new ways to make money.

Some people are partially retired/partially working and spending time exploring their passions, from art to travel to hobbies. Some people say they never will retire. And they don't. But they may slow down a bit and sprinkle in a bit more travel or other activities, perhaps family-related. Life perspective inevitably changes as time goes on and priorities change.

Rebooting and Reinventing

Whatever shape it takes, retirement—the "R" word—is a rebooting. It's a new start, with new purpose and energy, a period with time to reassess. It's a new adventure and the glass should be at least half full. In our book *Reboot Your Life: Energize Your Career and Life by Taking a Break,* we talk about stepping out of work by taking a Reboot Break (another word for a sabbatical or career break), then coming back better than ever. This retirement rebooting has those same aspects, as people step out of their full-time career:

* **Catching up with oneself** by clearing space mentally and physically.

* **Reconnecting** with people and favored, perhaps neglected, activities and places.

* **Exploring** new options and starting down new paths.

* **Being more creative** and passionate about how one's time is spent.

* **Being secure in who you are** in this new lifestyle you are designing.

* **Living the life you want!**

The reinvention comes all along the way, as you explore who you want to be, whether it's with new work to continue to earn money or hobbies. Did you ever say, as we have, that you are still figuring out what you want to do when you grow up? Reinvention allows you to explore this question and see what makes you feel relevant and inspired and fulfilled during your next stage. Try again what you used to do. Coaching kids' sports? Violin? Painting? Woodworking? Try something new. Yoga anyone? Learning a language? Gardening? Writing? Photography? Bowling? Causes?

Reinvention can also mean a new place to live, a new and healthier body, a new partner in life, a new outlook on life, a new way to relate to others. It isn't just doing new things.

Baby Boomers always wanted to make the world better. With thousands retiring every day, think of the creative energy that can be unleashed as people move into a new lifestyle with more time for ideas and new efforts. Even those who work every day now to make the world a better place can look forward to marrying their talents and passions with new causes calling for their attention. **Chapter 5: What Will I Do With My Time?** covers rebooting and reinventing, and has many ideas about how to spend time in volunteer and creative endeavors.

Transition

It's a transition. It may be several transitions as you wind down from regular work and wind up on you. That's right—you can be the designer and star of your story now, probably more so than in decades. There may be an unease to that, to taking time for yourself or focusing more on yourself, but you deserve it. Give yourself permission.

Ultimately, transition results in renewal. Author William Bridges describes three stages of transition, all of which resonate here. The first step is "letting go." It involves realizing that a phase of life is over, and you are moving away from it and into something else. Second is a "neutral zone," an in-between time of self-examination and discovery. This can be an empty and lonely time, or a very creative time, or both. The third stage is "beginning again," with all the attendant uncertainty and exhilaration.

Transition can be difficult for anyone because change is difficult. It is normal to feel emotional and even at a loss, especially in the beginning. People mourn—even if they don't realize it—leaving behind a job and its schedule and built-in network and way of life. It can take time to adjust.

It can be especially hard if retirement was forced upon you earlier than you planned, as in Gene's story.

Gene, an executive, felt betrayed when he was suddenly forced to retire without even being included in the decision-making. He was mad, sad, and confused. He mourned the job loss for six months. Then he began to take control with specific steps, including signing up for training to do taxes and attending our Reboot Your Life Retreat. At the end of a year, he had re-geared his life to a new norm in which he does people's taxes as a volunteer and is on the advisory board of a small company. He has reduced his expenses by moving to a smaller house, and he took an RV trip to see family and reconnect to himself. He says, "Life is good."

Practicalities of Transition

Several major themes relate to the practicality of transition. Retirees—whatever they are doing once they leave the full-time professional structure on which they have depended and in which they have functioned—ask, *"Where's the IT desk?"* They also ask about the support they need from bankers to brokers, career advisors and mentors, health and wellness experts, and more. In short: *"Where is my support team?!"* We suggest building your own advisory Team of Experts, and we offer ideas and resources throughout the book.

Also on practicality, we address Retirement Robbers and other challenges that can keep you from living a fulfilling and meaningful life. It may be startling to realize that this starts with you and your difficulty in saying "no" to the many opportunities that will come your way outside of what you really want to do. So, **Chapter 6: Retirement Robbers and Other Challenges** sorts through the kinds of challenges that arise when someone goes to a more flexible schedule and suddenly everyone wants a piece of that freer time—plus there is one's own propensity to procrastinate.

Naturally, your life involves others—especially if you live with someone—and you will take that into account. Often couples enjoy this time together more than they have for many years. There are new challenges (*Whose kitchen is this, anyway?*), but also many new opportunities for growth together and separately, as addressed in **Chapter 7: Renegotiating Life at Home.**

Health, Anticipating Change, and Legacy

We have referred to phases of retirement because, of course, retirement is not a monolith—the same from beginning to end. It will evolve as our life and circumstances change. Take health, for example. As we age, our capabilities, needs, desires, and challenges change, and we need to adapt.

Most importantly, we need to work on keeping—or restoring—our health, both physically and mentally. It should be a priority every day. **Chapter 8: Most Important of All: Your Health** addresses how to take charge of your health and some of the issues surrounding health. Some of these topics are uncomfortable, but we address them in this book to be comprehensive and realistic. You will want to address them, too, as you dream and plan what you want to do, and where and how you want to live.

We need to plan as best we can, but live in the time we are in. We need to anticipate the natural changes that will occur. Climb mountains while you physically can. Save the cruises for later.

We also talk about legacy, devoting **Chapter 9: Leaving Your Legacy** to it. Boomers want to leave a legacy of themselves and their families. It can take the form of family history and ethics, bricks and mortar, scrapbooks, or whatever you choose. It relates to telling your story.

Simplifying Life and Living With Passion

This brings us to the final theme in the book: Part of the gift of this new chapter of our lives is being able to simplify life and live a life of passion. Throughout the transitions and phases, there will be a natural downsizing—of workload, of material things, perhaps of living space. One begins to emphasize relationships and experiences even more than before, and more than possessions. It is part of clearing out and making room for this new stage to evolve. Living more simply can be a necessity for some, but a real benefit and pleasure for all.

Living a life of passion is the underlying goal of rebooting and reinventing. Passion—that is, doing things you love and value—is the driving force for a good life. It need not be seen as selfish, as it can include serving others in small ways and large as you follow your dreams. **Chapter 10: Simplifying Your Life and Living a Life of Passion** addresses ways to live a simpler, balanced life with attention to your passion and the priorities you set.

Using This Book

We hope this will be a guidebook for you to visualize, plan for, and navigate the next few decades successfully and meaningfully. Follow us through these pages as we help you on your next journey—one that you design.

The Retirement Boom is written to enable you to skip around to chapter topics and exercises. The Appendix, supplemented by our Website (*www.revolutionary-retirement.com*), is a treasure trove of resources. We encourage you to use this book as your companion, advisor, and support group in thinking about what you want to do to plan and live your own revolutionary retirement!

And now, back to basics. Next is an exercise to help you answer a preliminary retirement readiness questionnaire. Then it's on to planning and designing.

✎ Exercise 1-1: Retirement Readiness Questionnaire Before Reading *The Retirement Boom*

For this and the other exercises at the end of each chapter, we suggest you write in a journal or a notebook.

Take the Retirement Readiness Questionnaire #1 in the Appendix.* You most likely will not know all the answers yet, but it will at least get you thinking about your own story and where you may want to take it from here.

- ☐ Invest some time in it, as it will get you started and help identify the questions that are important to you.

- ☐ Then, you may want to go back and look at your questionnaire again after reading this book.

*The Appendix refers to some printable documents online, which are available at *www.revolutionary-retirement.com/private*. The password is revolutionary.

CHAPTER 2

Planning and Designing Your Reinvention

There is nothing like a dream to create the future.

—Victor Hugo

"Luck is the residue of design and desire," said Branch Rickey, the innovative executive of the Brooklyn Dodgers, many years ago. He had it right. We can create our own good luck by defining what we desire and putting plans in place to make it happen, or come pretty darn close. But if we don't have a vision or plan, we may end up someplace else entirely, and not of our choosing.

This chapter is about launching your next phase of life in a direction that is designed by you. It is meant to inspire you, give you practical tips on figuring out what is important to you, and help you identify what steps you need to get there. Subsequent chapters expand on the planning theme and many of the points here.

Thinking About Your Retirement

Many chafe at the word "retirement" and resist it. *Don't push me. Not so soon.* Accounting firms, among other service organizations, have mandatory retirement, usually at ages 58 to 60. The government allows us to begin drawing Social Security at age 62. But those ages still feel young, especially if you love what you are doing, are in good health, and live an active lifestyle. Despite the external pressures, we have our own internal clocks, like the beginning of a new year, which tell us it is time for a change—a change in how we live, work, and play.

As you hit whatever number it is for you that sparks a desire to stop working or to start working differently, planning for your next chapter is critical to guarantee that it will be as you envision it. For most of us, this is one of the best times of our lives. Our age and experience give us a kind of freedom from convention. It is time to do as we wish. We are in charge.

For some, this stage may be prematurely initiated by their company, creating some stress and anxiety because they haven't had a chance to plan ahead either emotionally or financially. However, they, too, can end up with a plan and take back the reins of control.

Many will tell you that the planning should have happened earlier, putting money away for this day or some day in the future. But it is never too late to plan. It takes time, thought, creativity, and sometimes taking a leap of faith. But you can achieve your dreams, even if you are just starting now!

So what is spurring you on to think about retiring? Is it your job or company? Everyone your age is leaving? Your partner or spouse is retired and wants you to "play" with him or her? A desire to do something else? Are you tired and need a rest? Have you been forced to retire? Or are you just ready for a change in what you do, how you do it, where you do it, and with whom you do it? You are not alone!

When Is the Right Time?

Timing is a result of many factors: age, financial resources, family desires and needs, and your personal goals.

A 2012 poll conducted by Associated Press–NORC Center for Public Affairs reported that 47 percent of older workers expect to delay retirement at least three years, increasing the average retirement age from 63 to 66. Eighty-two percent of people polled felt that they will continue to work for pay during retirement. Of course, money is often *number one* in everyone's mind. Can you afford to retire from your current position and try something new? Or can you retire and not have to have additional income? Most people seek financial advice before retiring. Hopefully, they have been working with those advisors for a while to build a plan. In the next chapter of this book, we talk through aspects of financial planning and give recommendations for maximizing what you have, and building a plan for what you need in your financial future.

The timing for leaving your current position might also be driven by:

* **Company policies.** Some companies have mandatory retirement ages or are downsizing.

* **Your benefits.** Some benefits may be at a higher rate if you wait to retire; others might be offered to retire early. This is happening as companies are looking for ways to cut costs or to bring in a new generation of employees, making room for Generation X and Millennials to move up into management positions.

* **Financial responsibilities.** Are your kids launched? Do you still have tuition to pay? Will your kids come back to live with you? Are your parents healthy and taken care of financially? Both of those generations may affect your planning.

* **Emotional readiness.** Sometimes even when we are driving toward a goal, we may feel melancholy about leaving the life and places where we have lived or the role we have had. It is normal and expected. Are you ready to let go of something in exchange for something else that you have longed for or planned?

You want to feel ready to make a change, not feel pushed to do so. Planning the timing is critical.

Getting Started: Envisioning Your Retirement

You are the writer of your story. Where you want the story to go is imagined and implemented by you, with the help of your friends and advisors.

We believe it starts with a vision. Envisioning success or where one hopes to be is a well-known technique in sports and other fields. We love the story of the athlete who won an Olympic bronze medal. When asked if there was anything he would do differently, he said somewhat sadly, "Although I envisioned myself winning a medal, I should have seen myself winning the gold." Famous Chinese pianist Liu Shih-kun was imprisoned for six years during the Cultural Revolution. He was forbidden to play a piano while in prison. Shortly after being released, he gave a fantastic concert—the best ever. "How did you do that without practice?" someone asked. He replied that, on the contrary, he had practiced every day in prison—in his mind.

So, there's power in envisioning. We suggest it for you in the form of an exercise that will help you to see an ideal future for yourself. It will get you working toward planning and reaching your goals. Every plan starts with a dream, a vision.

Visualizing: The Walking Meditation

To assist you in getting to a place in your mind that will focus on what you really want and need from your life going forward, we recommend the process of visualizing while walking. The combination of movement while you are thinking allows the mind to shift from the left side of the brain to the right side, enabling you to think more creatively and to be open to, and consider, new possibilities. We recommend taking a 30-minute walk in a calm and peaceful place, such as a park or by the water—somewhere where you won't be distracted. Ask yourself two questions: *What elements would I love to have as part of this next phase of life that will satisfy my heart and soul? How would I like to spend my time?* Imagine you are there, in that space. Assume for this exercise that you have no constraints, no financial concerns, no family to care for, and so forth.

Spend at least 30 minutes allowing your mind to go to a place that allows it to stretch and imagine the ideal. How does it feel? Make a point of not talking to anyone while on the walking/visualization exercise. Later, when you return to a place where you can write, get those ideas down in a journal or planning book, uncensored. Writing will help to solidify what you imagined. These are the thoughts that come from deep within you and can be foundational to what you want to do. Do not be surprised if those thoughts impact your emotions.

Write it Down

Another way to find and solidify your dreams and goals is by journaling. Putting pen to paper is a way to start to turn dreams into reality. Journaling about your process, ideas, dreams, and thoughts right from the start is an excellent way to capture fears and wishes—both significant parts of the planning process. Maybe you already write in a journal daily, or maybe you never have. Whatever the case, grab your journal or a handy notebook—or go out and buy a blank book or our *A Journal for Inspiration* (available on Amazon.com). Then sit in a quiet place to think and write. The first thing in the morning when you are close to dream time is the best. Try to write two to three pages a day.

Research has proven that writing by hand, as opposed to using a computer, makes people more creative and focused, and they retain better what they have written. Whichever is your preferred mode, put your thoughts down where you can think further about them and explore them with personal advisors. This will help you see past the resistance, fears, and negative thinking that can sometimes prevent dreams from becoming reality.

A journal is also a handy tool for jotting down information and ideas as they occur during the day, especially during a planning process like the one you are undertaking. You will have so many ideas, Websites to explore, and questions that need to be recorded, so keep your journal or a little notebook handy.

Identifying Goals and Getting Help

Like a business plan, your personal plan should start by setting goals and objectives. Here are some preliminary steps you might take in identifying your major goals and outcomes:

* **Think and daydream** about your next chapter, building on the visualization exercise.

* **Write about it**, which makes it more real. What does it look like? What would you like to be doing?

* **Talk about it to others,** especially your loved ones, to get reinforcement.

- **Seek help from a financial advisor** to understand where you stand.
- **Speak to your human resources department** to find out your retirement benefits and options, including timing.
- **Write down steps to take** toward achieving your dreams.
- **Begin researching and making plans.**

How Can Your Company Help?

More companies are realizing that, with 35 percent of the workforce retiring, they should have some new plans in place to support this employee population. Regardless of whether you have worked for your current company for 40 years or four years, find out what benefits it offers to people who are planning a new chapter. Because of the sheer numbers, many companies are investing in retirement planning to support their employees. It might be in the form of explaining the benefits to which you are entitled, giving advice about timing, offering a financial advisor to help you decide what to do with any profit-sharing or 401(k) plans you might have, or even training. It is still up to you, but you would be remiss not to look into and take advantage of all that is available. It is expected that you will seek this information, and many companies have people whose job it is to help make the transition smoother for you and for the company.

Pre-Retirement Planning: Take a Break to Plan and Design

Now that you have a vision, more information, and some ideas about goals, you can plan and design your next chapter. This takes time and thought and, sometimes, trying it out. Ahead, we discuss some approaches that many have found useful in preparing to create the lifestyle they want.

Pre-Retirement Reboot Break

The best way to do pre-retirement planning is to take a break from work. It is a "gift of time." All of us at this stage need time to clear our heads—to step back and think and plan for the retirement phase of life. It is difficult to plan for retirement while in the throes of working life and normal routine. Stress is high; time is in short supply. One's head is filled with logistics, details, scheduling conflicts, decision-making, and other pressures from work and home. E-mail, texting, and other electronic delights demand our attention and energy at all hours of the day and night. There's no space in our heads for dreaming, envisioning, or planning. If we do find a moment, it's likely to be only a little daydreaming or quick-caught computer time to Google trips or places to live. Then back to the reality of working. No, you need to take the time to step back and give time to your future.

If you can do it, taking a pre-retirement planning break two to five years before retirement is ideal. And you can take more than one such break to plan. As with any Reboot Break, it is a chance to open yourself to possibilities. Taking several months is recommended, but even one month can work, if you plan it right. For example, you might trade your house for one in a foreign country or another state to try out living in the area. Or you might do a one-month internship in a new career area or take selected classes.

Some people try something or someplace new for a short time and then decide whether they want to pursue the activity on a more sustained basis or reconsider what they want. Other concepts to explore might include the financial resources you will need, how the office will get along without you, whether you can handle being alone for a period of time, and ways of overcoming feelings of guilt from not working.

When Cathy took her pre-retirement break, she traded houses to spend a month in Italy. It went so smoothly with her staff while she was away that she realized they could handle things quite well in her absence. When she implemented her dream of working only three days a week, it gave her, and them, the confidence to know it was going to work. During this break, she also finalized her plan to move from Washington, DC to Santa Fe to concentrate on her consulting company and to become involved in the community.

Here's some advice about planning Pre-Retirement Reboot Breaks:

* **Plan ahead** so the break is really worthwhile. Figure out how to make it happen.

* **Take as long as you can** to realize the maximum benefit.

* **Get away from normal chores and routines, and test the waters.** You can do this for at least part of the time.

* **Involve your family in the planning and—if it fits the plan—in the pre-retirement break itself.** Communicating with, and including your loved ones, at least in the planning is key to success.

* **Be creative without spending huge amounts of money.** For example, some people trade houses or apartments, or house sit. The web can be helpful in identifying opportunities. Or do a staycation and explore near home.

* **If it's only a month, you can do a lot in a month.** It's twice the time of a two-week vacation and twice the opportunity to get away from it all and relax or try something new.

Mini Pre-Retirement Break

Is even a month too long for now? Take a long weekend, or a week, to unplug from your smart phone and computer and be alone with no schedule. It offers a small test of what it would be like to be away from all of that stimulation and structure. A mini pre-retirement sabbatical can also test the logistical and emotional planning required with one's family or significant other.

Unplugging can be the hardest part. Telling your office and others ahead of time that you are not going to be available electronically is a good idea. Then you need to try to stick to that plan to get the most out of your time off.

Other Ways to Plan by Trying Something New

Not everyone can take a long career break to envision retirement, and there are other effective ways to do so.

Think about what you want your life to look like. Consider all aspects. Explore possibilities, such as where to live, types of volunteering, how to use your skills, new interests (classes or workshops to take), different types of books to read, new places to travel, and how to weave it all together in a way that defines you better than simply being "retired." You may not want to do all those activities right away, but you might start thinking about what they could be. Another way is to do the envisioning, then put it into practice on vacations. Such could be the case with volunteering, or in prepping to move to a new place.

Linda and Larry had busy, successful careers in Washington, DC—she as a university administrator, he as a trade association executive. They bought a home in Santa Fe several years before they planned to retire. As much as possible, they took vacations there in different seasons to get an idea of what life would be like and to meet new friends. In a way, they practiced retirement, and they also reaffirmed that Santa Fe was right for them. When they retired, they sold their DC house and packed up for Santa Fe, then settled into their new community and life. They reveled in the freedom, explored their surroundings, met new friends, deepened older friendships, and had a wonderful time. In many ways, it felt like "coming home" to them.

Post-Retirement Recalibration

If you are already retired, you can take time to add activities or a whole new way of life, including a new career, you might not have anticipated. Often retirees want to reset their lives after being retired awhile. Labeling this process as a recalibration and setting a time frame for assessment and planning will help you in discovery of new options and making a decision. It is never too late to take a Reboot Break. The Break can give you new insights into what you want and need to do to reinvent or revolutionize your life.

Peter, based in Los Angeles, had been the head of the financial advisory services division of a Big Four accounting firm. He happily retired and pursued some of the leisure activities he hadn't been able to do when working long hours six days a week, with heavy travel, throughout his career. He thought he was fulfilled by being involved on nonprofit boards when he retired. Within a year, though, he was back working, although unpaid, as chair of his state's Investment Council, where his expertise and audit skills were sorely needed. Fortunately, he recognized what he needed to feel relevant and fulfilled and recalibrated. Not only is he happy with what he is doing, it is a gift to the state to have a person of his caliber doing this civic duty.

Key Questions in Planning

Here are several things to consider as you plan for what is next.

Where Do You Want to Live?

This is a time in people's lives when they consider changing the way they have lived or finding a way to live even better than they have before, as Linda and Larry did. It could be simplifying or downsizing or "living light" in a smaller place, or in a different town or country. It sounds daunting, but thousands of people have pulled up stakes and moved into the city, out of the city, to another state, and in some cases, to another country to find a new lifestyle. Thousands have moved to Mexico, Costa Rica, Florida, and other less-expensive destinations, dramatically reducing their cost of living. Those who moved discovered a way to live that they had not imagined before because their research educated them about the possibilities. They spent time in these new places and tested them out, often during a pre-retirement break. Then, knowing their desires, they could plan ahead for the move.

Alan and Nancy began planning 10 years ahead for retirement and knew they needed to move to a less-expensive place to live. Through explorations, they found a county in rural Kentucky that appealed to them. Keeping an eye on real estate through two local newspapers, they found a perfect lot to buy seven years before retirement. Then, over several years, they camped there in the summer. They came to know the community and made new friends, including a couple that "adopted" this outsider couple. Five years before, they designed the new home they would build and where they now live in more space at a fraction of the expense of their former life on Long Island. They love it!

Questions to Consider When Deciding Where to Live

Do you want to:

* Live in a less-expensive city?

* Stay in your current home or downsize?

* Be part of a specific community/relocate near activities you love?

* Try a new climate or lifestyle?

* Move closer to family?

* Move to your vacation home?

* Move overseas and create a new lifestyle?

The AARP Website (*www.aarp.org*) is one of the best resources out there for anyone over 50. Truth be told, the site is good for any adult, at any age. When exploring where to live, you'll find list upon list of places to consider, with such interesting categories as healthiest, most affordable, or best places for singles.

With Whom Do You Want to Spend Time?

Maintaining social connections can be challenging throughout our lives. The loss of work friends is the most unforeseen challenge of retirement. It's important to take an active role in building and maintaining your support network of friends, family, and acquaintances when you retire. Those in your network should be supportive, positive, and nurturing; teach you new things; and be fun to be with. Build the enrichment of this network into your plan ahead of time wherever possible. Old friends will welcome you back into their lives; current relationships will need to be nurtured, including family. It is important for you to make time for relationships before you retire.

Think about who is in your life now and who else you would like to add.

Family

How far away are your parents, siblings, children, and grandchildren? They become important parts of this life chapter, so you need to think about how much time you want to plan around them and, importantly, what they require of you. The answers may entail moving or more frequent travel. Many Baby Boomers are faced with aging parents, so being nearby or able to travel to spend time and to care for them is important.

When you are with parents, children, and grandchildren, what activities do you like to do together? What can you plan in advance to do?

New Friends

Many who have focused mainly on their careers find themselves with few and, in some cases, no friends outside of work. Married couples and partners often rely on each other, as there is little time for anything else. So cultivating new friendships becomes a big part of retirement or next-chapter planning. Tap into the friends of your friends or of your spouse or partner. Be proactive and make a plan to get together for coffee or an activity you would like to do with these people. You will be surprised how responsive people are to a new experience and stepping out of their comfort zones, as well. It is especially important if you are moving to a new place where you don't already have a set of supportive friends.

A good way to meet new friends is to consider taking classes that interest you or joining a professional association or local club, place of worship, activity center, or travel group. Some people we interviewed organized potluck dinners and asked guests to invite one person no one knew to introduce them to the group. Everyone benefitted. Start expanding your circle of friends before you retire or make it a priority now. It may mean stepping out of your comfort zone.

If you are single, participation in online dating Websites for people over 55 has skyrocketed. Reports from many are that it is an easy and fast way to meet people for dating and companionship. You need to test it out or talk to people to find the more reputable sites. Many people use it to build pen pal relationships with people across the country.

The key is finding people who support your dream and your vision. You want to surround yourself with happy, positive people. It is a choice we can all make. Seek out people who live an active, interesting, healthy lifestyle and who will encourage and support your doing the same.

Where Do You Dream of Traveling?

One of the first things that most people talk about when they retire is traveling. We know several people who actually lived their dream, bought an RV, and traveled across the country. They had countless memorable experiences that are revisited as they continue to travel throughout the years.

Travel can provide a renewed sense of self, a view of the world that sparks us to think and act differently, almost always for the better. It can provide solitude or it can create the opportunity for companionship, sharing the experience with a friend or loved one. Most of us travel for either adventure or for relaxation. The possibilities are endless.

When thinking about travel you might want to consider:

* **Possible destinations:** United States, overseas, historical sites, places from your roots, homes of friends or family, places you've always wanted to see.

* **With whom you want to travel:** spouse or partner, friends, children, tour groups.

* **How much traveling you want to do:** number of trips each year, duration.

* **Different ways to travel:** bicycle, motorcycle, bus, river cruise, motor home.

Linda had a long and very demanding career in the Foreign Service, as did her husband, Leo. They spent most of their time living overseas and rarely got to travel within the United States. Leo retired first and together they made plans for the day Linda could take the plunge. They had many plans but one was to travel the country, so Leo bought a compact RV with all of the bells and whistles. Now they drive the RV to visit family or friends once a month. They are finally seeing the country and enjoying the journey together.

How Else Do You Want to Fill Your Time?

Chapter 4: Reinventing Into New Work and **Chapter 5: What Will I Do With My Time?** are the go-to sources for ideas and resources on working and non-working possibilities.

Planning by Decade

As part of being the designer or reinventor, you might approach your planning by what you will want and need in each of the next decades of your life. Some of this you cannot know, but it is good to keep in mind as you think ahead. Two major areas are your activities and where you live.

Activities

Aging is being redefined. We are able and interested in having new experiences and adventures much longer in life. However, our capabilities likely will change with each decade. The longer we keep our bodies moving and our minds active, the better, but we might want to get all of the physically challenging plans into the first years of retirement—whether we are still working or not—and more cruising, visiting friends and family, reading, and coursework into the next years as our bodies slow down. Go on a bicycle tour now, and take a cruise to Alaska, the Bahamas, Hawaii, or Bermuda later. Travel rigorously now and continue learning with courses later, like Annette.

At 85, Annette is taking a new course of study at a local university through Quest, a lifelong learning program in New York City organized by a group of retirees. She attends classes four times a week and is even learning a new language. There she has met many new friends with common interests and looks forward each week to the structure, learning, and mental challenges the course provides with fun and interesting people. Mind you, Annette still travels too, but these courses keep her active between trips!

Because there are so many of us Baby Boomers, a huge array of options has been developed to provide us with learning opportunities, travel, and experiences to keep us healthy, vital, and young. See what is happening where you live or where you want to live. The main idea is to think ahead, being both realistic and positive. How might you anticipate what you will need now and in the future?

Where You Live Over Time

Earlier in this chapter, we talked about where you would live when you retire—mainly whether you would move to a different residence or city. The question here is how that might change over time: How might your living needs and preferences change over the next 10, then 20 years? You may live in a house now but in 10 years want to be in a condo or apartment that would require less physical maintenance by you. You may have a garden now and want only balcony plants later. You may have stairs now, but need to be on one floor because of knee problems later. At some point, you might need to move to independent or assisted living, or have lots more help at home. Downsizing is a matter of preference, but at some point it becomes more imperative.

> *Jaye rents an apartment in New York City and owns a house on Long Island. At this time, she works in the city, with a very active life of walking everywhere, and spends weekends at her house. Her plan for the next 10 to 15 years is to move from the hectic city life to her house in the country. Though it requires quite a bit of maintenance, she is willing to hire or have someone live there to help over time so she can stay in the house for the next several decades. She'll likely do more driving for errands, and she may spend more time at home later in life than she does now. In the meantime, she is getting the house ready for her, and perhaps others, to live there full time.*

If we plan now for the type of housing we want, the friends who might serve as a "community" for us, and the places we might live to enrich our lives decade by decade, we will have more fulfilled lives.

Think About Your Bucket List

Consider what experiences and destinations you have in mind—and think about when you would like to do them. The book *1,000 Things to See Before You Die* is a great inventory of interesting places. It is not everything, but just looking through it can stir up ideas that you might not otherwise have considered. You may want to return to experiences you had when you were younger, or try things you have always imagined. Recently a woman decided that for her 70th birthday she wanted to sky-dive. Many of us are not that adventurous, but maybe fly fishing, golfing at St. Andrews in Scotland, taking a photography workshop, scuba diving, or even skiing for the first time would do. Most of us have something we would like to try and have never had the time for. Why not have fun planning for it now?

Writing down your bucket list might help you discover things you are forgetting to include in your planning. Remember to keep that journal of all of the ideas that pop into your head from this book, conversations with friends, and your own reading and research.

Don't Plan Alone—Communicate!

To help you plan, it is critically important to talk to those around you who care and want you to have the best possible life. Including them in your thinking will give you new ideas, support those you have, and help you understand your loved ones' hopes and fears for your retirement. The more inclusive you are, the less likely they are to be naysayers. You want and need their support. Celebrate the possibilities with them, even if they're not necessarily included in everything. If your family and friends feel a part of it, you will get less resistance and more support. Here are a few suggestions:

✱ **Include the people who will be affected by a retirement/ transition** in the decision process early on to create a smoother transition. They can be sounding boards and challenge you to think more—or less—broadly. Fearing the reaction of others, and thus avoiding those potentially difficult conversations, will cause more problems than dealing with it up front in a calm and confident way. If you are convinced of your decision, others will get on board more quickly, especially if you ask for their help and ideas. If you receive some pushback from naysayers or those who are anxious, don't let them rain on your parade.

✱ **Mutually share goals and expectations with your spouse or partner** to find alignment and build a plan that suits both of you. What activities do you want to do together? What do you want to do separately? Having that open and healthy conversation will ignite a spark that will inspire you both.

✱ **Be sure your children are part of the conversation,** once you are clear and have a plan. They will want to know what to expect and also what you expect of them. At the same time, you can seek their suggestions. Maybe they were planning on built-in babysitters and you were planning to live abroad!

✱ **Do talk to your friends,** as, more often than not, they will provide just the encouragement, support, and ideas you need.

Anticipate and Plan for Risk Factors

There are risks to living longer. As you think about where you will live and what you will do, you will obviously be thinking about how much money you will need. Planning for a longer life span, rather than a shorter one, will help to avert the risk of not having enough money, not living in the right place, or not having the right support around you. You will need to plan for your physical and mental well-being and make sure you will be in a nurturing environment. That is clearly important throughout life but will be more critical as you slowly come to rely on others more than in the past.

Health is another risk factor over which we have more control than we may think. Whatever we do physically helps us mentally as well. Not doing any kind of exercise not only shortens our lives, but also our mental capacity. However, even if we plan to exercise and eat healthily, physical ailments can throw a wrench in our planning. Plan for the limitations of Medicare or other benefits you have now or will need later, like long-term care insurance.

There are many financial risk factors to anticipate. These will be discussed in the next chapter.

Another unexpected twist can be suddenly having to become a caregiver to others, which can curb your finances, as well as your ability to do some of the things you planned. This isn't something you can plan for. It's just something that happens.

We must plan as much as we can with all of the knowledge and information we can gather. Sometimes unexpected things come our way. Be prepared to adjust plans as needed. Keeping a positive attitude and being open to what comes your way will help to make the journey throughout your next chapter a smoother ride.

Build Your Team of Experts: Where's the Technology Desk?

In retirement, you have new challenges because you are missing some of the support you had before. Like the IT help desk person who would come running when you had a computer question, or the people who always knew how to do spreadsheets, formats, PowerPoint, or whatever you needed. Now, you are on your own and realize that you need IT support plus advice on lots of other things in life, from health to finances to travel to building a new business. You need your own "advisory board." And you now need or still need support like a pet sitter, house sitter, snow removal, or relocation services.

We call it your "Team of Experts." The members likely will vary as you move through your plan to reach your dreams and goals. Chances are you already have some of your team in place—at least we hope so. They can be friends, family, colleagues, someone in a barter situation, or someone you hire. You need to decide in each case what help you need and whether it is something for which you want to pay. Often that is a sensible solution. Hours spent struggling on your own can be costly in time, frustration, and stress.

No one can do it all alone. In fact, the most successful people in life are those who know where to go to get the support and resources they need.

Technology Support

In interviewing hundreds of people, we always heard up-front about the need for technology assistance—people who can get information and data organized, who know how to use certain technologies and how to fix what isn't working. Even if you are computer savvy, trust us, problems will occur, and you, too, will be asking yourself, *"Where's the IT desk?"*

Other examples of tech issues are setting up your home Wi-Fi, or syncing the computer and television, or getting the printer to work. Or figuring out your new smart phone. Or figuring out how to communicate on Skype or other venues. Or advice on keeping track of all your passwords!

It's prudent to know whom you can call for the services and resources you need before the panic sets in.

You may have friends who are experts. Teens have become the best technical advisors to Baby Boomers. Jaye's 14-year-old niece Kasey is her expert. Local colleges and high schools may have job boards where people advertise their services. And don't forget the Geek Squad and, of course, Apple's Genius Bar. Or other customer support programs that are available free or can be purchased.

Paul, a former chief information officer, shared:

Soon after retirement, an old friend of mine invited me to provide some consulting for his company. "Send me your proposal and fees this week," said David. I was thrilled but in sheer panic. I know this sounds crazy, but I didn't know how to type a proposal including a pricing table. I could talk about mainframes and big-picture issues. Then I had staff around me for IT help. My administrator could whip up this type of proposal in minutes. I went to the Apple store, where you can sign up to work on your own personal project for two hours. Within a short time, I had created a professional-looking letter proposal and learned how to attach it to an e-mail.

New technology comes out every week. A big change is tablets with Microsoft Office so everything can be done on a lighter, smaller platform. Your advisors can help you stay up to date on changes that benefit you. You also can take advantage of online training.

Getting your IT needs supported will give you the foundation you need to launch into all of your other plans. See the Appendix for further technology assistance resources.

Planning the Team

Build into your plan for your revolution and evolution a list of what and whom you will need to support you. There's a template in the Appendix to get you started. Make an honest assessment of what you can and can't do yourself. Sometimes we don't even know there are people who help in areas we need. Perhaps you will need legal help, for example, in starting a new business, or a specialist in dealing with an emotional loss, or an expert to help you launch and market a new idea. None of us are good at everything. Who and what is missing from your plan? Include building the team in your goal setting.

The Appendix also has extensive resources, by category, to assist you in finding information, tools, and support in all aspects of planning for your next chapter.

Integration: The Circle Goals Exercise

Here is one of our ways to get you thinking and building a plan that will take you to the place you dream about. Now you have a vision; let's get the goals on paper.

Often the New Year's resolutions that we write are forgotten two weeks later, possibly because they are not realistic or do not relate to real life. Then we go right back to our old habits, whether they are about our health, finances, relationships, or work, thus sustaining lives that are not balanced, and are therefore, unfulfilling. The Circle Goals Exercise is about changing your life and putting it back into harmony and balance.

In the exercise section of this chapter, we're going to ask you to complete Circle Goals that will serve as your guidepost for integrating all aspects of your life. Cathy created this activity and used it for several years before we wrote about it in our books *Reboot Your Life* and *Revolutionary Retirement*.

The purpose of the exercise is to balance your life around its most important aspects for the coming year and to move you closer to realizing your dreams. The simple chart is a circle divided into six or eight pie slices of equal size to remind you to give equal time—at least mental thought—to them. It's a holistic approach.

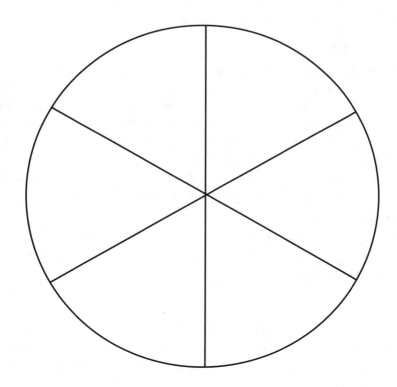

Label the pie slices on the chart with six key aspects of your life. Examples might be: career, financial, travel, philanthropy, spirituality or religion, creativity, friends and family, romantic relationships, health and exercise, or whatever you want to realize over the next year. The categories may be for that year only, such as renovate your house, or ongoing, such as health and exercise.

Once you have decided on the categories, write five goals for each one that are measurable and obtainable in the year. Make them specific, such as "redo my financial budget in the next three months" or directional, as "travel to a place I am interested in moving to, within the next year." You should be able to sit down and know at the end of the year whether you met the goals or not.

Here are some example categories, followed by an example of one category with specific goals:

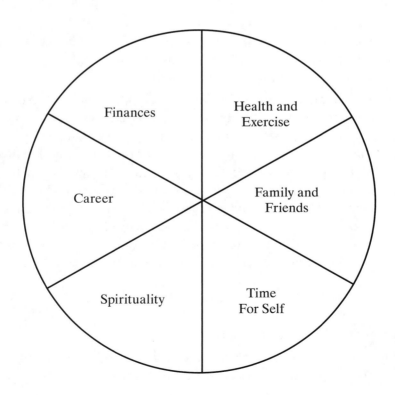

Finances:

- ☐ Enter all financial records into a software program in the next three months.

- ☐ Read a book on retirement financial management in the next four months.

- ☐ Make a list of where I can cut back and plan a budget within two months.

- ☐ Meet with a financial planner by mid-year.

- ☐ Pay off credit card balances each month.

It may take you a couple of hours, or even days, to come up with five goals for each category, but it is important to do so, to stretch yourself. When you are finished, go back and pick out one goal from each category that is most important for you to do of the five in that category and put those on another circle. This circle, with the top goal in each category, is one you might carry with you and refer to every once in a while.

"I recommend putting the larger chart, with five goals each, away for six months, then reviewing it," Cathy says. "Don't try to update or change it. Just look at it and see where you are against your goals. It is at the end of the year that you want to take the time to reflect."

We have learned from doing this over time that most people accomplish much more of their goals because they have taken the time to think about them and write them down. Secondly, the process makes you think about all aspects of your life and try to keep them in more balance. By having the five goals in each category you really do have a way to make things happen in many areas of your life. And that is what makes us happy: acknowledging the fullness and complexity of our life and taking the time to realize and enjoy it. By spending mental, as well as physical, time on what we want from life, we are more in control of how we realize those goals. We call it being present and open to what synchronicity comes our way.

Planning Grid: Turning Goals Into Action

For those who want a further tool for more detailed planning, we offer the Action Planning Grid in the Appendix as a way to organize your thinking around each goal you want to achieve during your next chapter. First, think about the bigger goals (i.e., building a long-lasting financial plan, improving your health, traveling, spending time with the family, learning something new). As you drill down in any one of those larger retirement dreams, you will need to think through the various steps to make them happen. With each goal in mind, what will you need to do first and then to build from there? Who can help you realize your goals, and by when?

Be as specific as possible, giving yourself timelines to ensure that you actually get it done. You can continue to add to the grid and change things as you learn from each step you take.

Overcoming Fears

Even with the best planning, emotional barriers can get in the way. Fears about finances or making the right decisions about where to live or continuing to work or how to be relevant may make the best-laid plans hard to set in motion. Josh said:

> *At long last, I had decided to retire after a long series of disappointments in my life and in work. I was full of excitement, but the fears started to set in. All the "what ifs" came flooding through my mind. I suddenly felt the one thing I had wanted for so long might be too hard to do. Then a friend gave me a quote by Henry Ford: "Whether you think you can or can't, you are right." So I decided that I can.*

That's the spirit. People work through their fears and anxieties in several ways. Some people find that surrounding themselves with supportive and positive people is a key to success. They learn to deflect negative internal voices or the reactions by naysayers to their vision for a new life. And they develop confidence by planning ahead.

The next chapter of your life is as important as all the others, but you have greater knowledge, more experience, and a clearer sense of who you are and what you want and need from life. Now you have to get those goals on paper and surround yourself with the necessary support to usher you through what needs to get done. Taking steps day-by-day toward your life's dreams will calm the jitters and keep the path clear for takeoff.

Keeping your goals in mind, you can explore the ideas and make choices. If your plan isn't working, that is okay, because you can always change it. Remember: You are writing your own story.

✎ Exercise 2-1: Circle Goals Exercise

❏ Draw your circle with six equal pie slices and categories.

❏ Put five goals under each category.

❏ Review it every six months.

❏ Create a second circle with just the categories and one key goal in each.

❏ Put that in your wallet or purse and look at it every once in a while.

❏ Have a cup of tea or glass of wine on next New Year's Day and go over your goals.

Congratulate yourself on what you have accomplished—60 to 70 percent of the list is terrific!

CHAPTER 3

Making Your Money Last

A penny saved is a penny earned.
—Benjamin Franklin and Grandma Kitty

Many of us grew up with parents or grandparents who lived through the Great Depression. Cathy's Grandma Kitty was one of them. She could boil a chicken with homemade noodles and serve 20 for Sunday dinner. She tore paper napkins in half to save money. And she saved every day until she died at age 86. The memory of the Depression was talked about much in the last recession—how people learned to make do with very little. Yet they found ways to be happy, to follow their passions, and to live well into older age. We hope to never face what our parents and grandparents did, but we still are concerned about money. What if we live to 100? Do we have enough for ourselves and our family to live the way we want? Can we fund our retirement, whenever we decide to quit working?

Welcome to the chapter that lays out some basics on making your money last! This is not your usual financial advice information, however, because we are not financial advisors, and there are many good ones out there. This chapter is designed to give you some commonsense approaches to managing money-related issues in your next chapter of life. It is written in a little different voice than the other chapters because there are so many facts and statistics we want to convey to you, so bear with us, please.

To live your dreams and follow your passions, you will need to think creatively. Once you can envision your next chapter and lifestyle, the next step is planning how to make that happen, financially. The timing and quality of your next few decades in life depends, to a great extent, on the resources and assets you have available or will be able to access.

Think of your personal resources as a basket of assets, physical and psychological, to manage. The most commonly thought of financial assets are the cash, stocks, bonds, mutual funds, gold, or other liquid assets you might have. Another set of tangible assets might be real estate or farmland you might own, as an asset, a rental, or other revenue-generating property. A third asset might be a business you own, or will develop, that brings in revenue or might have value when sold, or the salary you make as an employee.

But the most important asset is really *you,* and the continued invest-ment in your skill sets, knowledge, experiences, and contacts throughout the rest of your life. This chapter is about how to understand and leverage those assets to live your dreams.

> *Bev was a practicing physician in California for many years. She wanted to cut back on her hours and was frustrated with the HMO and healthcare systems in the state. She went back, at age 60, to get a master's in public health at University of California at Los Angeles (UCLA) to both understand the flaws in the system and be able to do other things with her education. Today she consults for hospitals on quality care of patients, at her own pace and time. She has time to spend with her kids and grandkids in Washington state and travel. She keeps her certification as a medical doctor current, just in case she needs it, but is happy to have more free time now. She is making a good income at age 67 and plans to continue through her 70s.*

Knowing your "financial and lifestyle facts"—the financial and other resources you have now, and will be able to access in the future—is criti-cal to your planning. Those "facts" include not just money, but housing, friends, business contacts, family obligations, health, skill sets, knowledge, educational background, work experience, and other considerations you want to understand as you design your next chapter. We will help you do that in the exercises in this book.

In writing this chapter, we offer you a creative way to look at building and maintaining the assets you have, as well as how to find ways of lowering your costs for the rest of your life. We have drawn upon the advice of a number of financial planners, people who have retired successfully and unsuccessfully, and our own experiences to bring you stories, examples, exercises, and wisdom from the experts.

We have all asked ourselves those middle-of-the-night questions: *Do I have enough? Will my kids ever be launched? Will my parents have to move in with me?* and *Who am I if I am not working full-time?* But what we really want to be thinking about are: *What are my passions? How do I live my dreams?* and *How do I fund those dreams?*

Everyone needs to have a financial foundation from which to build his or her plan. You will need financial advisors or someone whom you trust and who has the expertise to guide you. Those advisors can help you assess what you have, what you need, what you can afford, and where the gap might be. They might include an accountant, a tax attorney, an estate attorney, an investment advisor, a certified financial planner, a credit counselor, or other people with specialized expertise. Ask your friends, employer, lawyer, and other trusted advisors whom they recommend. Interview everyone and find someone you trust. Ask for referrals and follow up. These advisors are the most important part of your Team of Experts.

The Financial Facts About U.S. Baby Boomers Nearing Retirement

Well, there is sobering news here. We won't dwell on it for long, but we all need to understand the "facts" to be able to manage the way we live our dreams. More than 67 percent of workers feel like they are behind in retirement savings, and 56 percent don't know how much they'll need for post-work years.

Roughly half of all workers do not have a retirement plan, and for most of those who do, the likely retirement benefit is $80 a month. This is why Social Security is, and will be, even more important as a source of retirement income for many and such a "hot potato," politically. A recent U.S. government study from 2012 says that only 25 percent of Baby Boomers are financially prepared for retirement. Many had thought the equity in their homes would be their savings, but that has disappeared, or greatly diminished.

In fact, many Boomers are delaying retirement for two key reasons: They want to stay relevant and active in their 60s, 70s, and 80s; and they also need to shore up their retirement funds after the financial recession of 2007–2012. According to a 2012 Bank of America Merrill Edge Report survey, 57 percent of respondents said they would delay retirement, compared to 44 percent the year before.

Andrew thought he had saved enough for early retirement at age 50, but the health issues of his wife and special educational needs of his daughter put pressure on him to create a new technology strategy consulting business targeted to large financial firms. Fortunately, he had left a large financial company as CIO, and that gave him credibility to consult. It wasn't what he planned, but he recalibrated and is consulting part-time to replenish his retirement funds.

The vision of retirement many of our parents enjoyed has become a fading dream, replaced by the harsh reality of declining private pensions, inadequate retirement savings, escalating healthcare costs, and mounting debt. Financial fear is the motivation for most, and that's why, according to the Bureau of Labor Statistics, the percentage of workers over 65 is increasing faster than any other age group.

Rising healthcare costs will hit us most as we age. A 2015 HealthView study, cited by AARP, finds the average couple will need $266,000 out-of-pocket, even with Medicare, to cover healthcare in retirement, not including long-term care.

During the 20th century, life expectancy grew by nearly three decades, and longevity gains are continuing. Average life expectancy in 2010 was 76.7, and is projected to be 79.2 in 2020 and 81.2 in 2040. If you are alive today at age 65 or older, your life span is expected to be at least to age 85. It is still the norm that women tend to live longer than men, but the gap is closing.

This new longevity, according to AARP, is not just about living longer, but also living better and maintaining a balanced, vital lifestyle. This will impact our attitudes and public policy positions on issues such as healthcare, financial security, care giving, and quality-of-life issues. The fastest-growing age group in the population is the 100-plus population, and the second-fastest is those over the age of 85.

According to AARP, there are three other significant trends that will impact income available for retirement:

* Seventy percent of AARP members still provide financial support for their kids, and 40 percent are helping support both their kids and grandchildren.

* By 2015, unmarried Boomers will account for 21 million households, or 46 percent of all Boomer households. Often these households are more vulnerable to financial and healthcare challenges.

* The number of age 75-plus households headed by single women is projected to grow from fewer than six million in 2010 to 13 million by 2050. Women in general have less savings for retirement because they earned less during their lifetimes.

Having these facts, we can address the problems head-on and make sure our plans adjust to face these realities. We must be adaptable as people, as well as a nation, and understand what we can do to live well as we grow older, as well as take care of those who cannot care for themselves.

So, enough of the concerning statistics! We have the ability to change the numbers as well as the impact. We just need to know the baseline from where we start. Our longevity and relatively good health create many new and exciting opportunities to continue our current careers and interests, as well as to have time to develop and follow new ones.

The Basics of Financial Planning and Budgeting—Or, Getting Your Stuff Organized!

Experts say you should have saved from eight times to 12 times your current household income to live comfortably in retirement. That means if your household income today is $80,000, you need savings of at least $640,000 to $960,000. That presumes you are drawing down on your savings and have little or no income beyond your savings, Social Security, or small pensions. What if you continue to work in some manner or have income, such as paid boards or rental property, or annuities from a small business? It can make all the difference in the world between getting by and following your dreams!

Think about your assets and the way you use them. You are not just relying on the liquid part of your savings (cash, stocks, bonds), but many financial planners don't take the rest into consideration. Here is an example:

> *Joyce was meeting with her financial planner to go over her portfolio, and the planner asked her risk appetite for stocks, because, at her age, many planners suggest more bonds. Joyce said she wanted more stock funds and the planner said, "But what if you need to draw down funds in the next 10 years?" Joyce said, "I sit on several corporate boards that have annuity-like fees until the age 72, so I do not plan to draw down any funds for the next ten years." Because the planner was only looking at liquid assets, she had not taken into account any other income. They then created a plan that took that into account.*

The planner's advice was based on a standard model offered by many institutions. Unfortunately, many planners, especially those associated with financial institutions, only want to focus on that one basket of liquid assets that they can invest for you, and make fees. *You* have to take charge of your "portfolio of assets" and be sure all assets are considered, not just those under the institution's current or potential management.

Take the MyMoneyCheckUp®

Let's face it: For most of us, the words *budgeting* and *financial planning* are anathemas. They mean hours of work, lots of details, and, sometimes, unpleasant surprises. But if we don't do the basics of financial planning, we will never understand what we need to fund, and live our dreams. So stay with us on this, and resolve to do it just this once. The first time is the hardest, but once you have done it and keep the information up to date, online or in paper format, you will have the freedom to spend your time dreaming and acting on, the things you most want to do. It can actually be fun! (Okay, maybe that's a little too strong a statement, but it is freeing once you do it!)

First, go to *www.mymoneycheckup.org/syff* and take the National Foundation for Credit Counseling (NFCC) MyMoneyCheckUp®. The NFCC is the 60 year-plus-year-old national association of non-profit accredited credit counseling agencies with more than 600 locations across the United States and in Puerto Rico. The NFCC member agency network provides financial literacy education and counsels millions of consumers a year, providing education and solutions around issues such as budgeting, debt, foreclosure mitigation, and bankruptcy.

More than 50,000 people have taken the MyMoneyCheckUp® across the country, and it gives you a baseline of where you are in understanding financial planning, budgeting, and the use of money in everyday life. Take the MyMoneyCheckUp® and set it aside to reflect on after you have finished this chapter.

Now fill out the Budgeting and Financial Records Worksheets, which are from a number of sources. The worksheets are available on our Website, *www.revolutionary-retirement.com*. There are other great resources and budgeting tools listed in the Appendix and on our Website. Ask your financial planners for their worksheets and guides, as well, to decide what works best for you.

Gather All Your Information

Now the not-so-fun part! The real issue is finding all of your data, files, account numbers, financial reports, tax returns, and so forth, and getting them all into the same file, electronically or physically. As you live longer, this gets more complicated, and often we forget about things—important information that our parents told us about their accounts or important papers we have misplaced. Or, if you are like some of us, the information is scattered across your house and office, in multiple files.

This is the hardest part of financial planning—being as thorough as possible in finding all the relevant information you need to think about for your next chapter. Because it doesn't just include financial stuff. It also includes wills and powers of attorney and other legal documents. It is also about organizing your resume and bio, your work records, your certifications and coursework, your health records, and addresses of relatives and close friends. It includes creating a new contact database for your future endeavors, whatever they may be, and listing people who can serve as your Team of Experts. There actually are some great software programs out there to help you with this, and they are listed in the Appendix. Also, try to break the sorting and gathering of information tasks down into smaller chunks, and involve your whole family.

Think about some reward that you will deserve once you get this done—an incentive beyond its being something you should do. Maybe a great dinner out or a weekend trip or a new laptop! Make it attractive enough to keep motivated.

Peter got his family to help find all the relevant information. Each member of the family was given a task. They did it over a period of a week and celebrated on the weekend with each one getting a wish fulfilled. There was a lot of laughter and complaining, but they got it done. It was a good lesson for the teenagers and a way for the family to bond. The reward was a dinner out to their favorite Mexican restaurant. The best result, however, was peace of mind for Peter and his wife.

Talk About It

Money is even more volatile than politics for discussions between spouses and partners, but if you can't talk about it, you may be on the road to disaster. Make money discussions a priority with your family. Talk to your spouse, partner, children, and parents about what your dreams and plans are, and how they relate to them. Find out what their dreams are, as well, and how everyone can find ways to fund them. Topics might include when you want to retire or leave your current position, when your spouse or partner wants to do the same, where you want to live, what kind of activities you want to engage in, what travel and other spending you plan, what education and career plans the kids have, and how you might budget. And it is a good time to make clear to your children when they are expected to be independent.

There may be some surprises during these talks. For example, your spouse or partner may want to retire right away and live near a golf course or a lake, and you want to move closer to the grandkids or live in a large city. You may want to start a new business, and your spouse or partner wants to travel around the United States in an RV. He or she might want to invest savings in a venture, and you fear you will run out of money if that fails. You may not want to, or be able to, retire at the same time, or, as is increasingly seen, your kids might want to move back home with you!

Joann's daughter and son-in-law asked to move in with her for awhile when they were changing jobs and looking for a house to buy. It was pretty comfy and the stay extended for more than a year, with no house on the horizon. Joann had a discussion with them about sharing the utility and food costs. To their credit, they willingly agreed, and it also gave them impetus to step up the house hunt. They just hadn't thought about the drain on their mother's retirement income.

What if I Don't Have Enough? 5 Ways to Make Your Money Last

The question of whether we have enough money is often the reason we don't take the time to get all our financial information organized. We are afraid of the answer, and that it might be "no." Never fear: There are many options open to you, and that is what we will discuss next. We suggest ways you can make up the difference between what you have and what you need to live the life you want. That is why having the facts is so important. If you understand the gap, you will be able to figure out things like how long to keep working or where you might find resources or how to reset expectations. It will help you set boundaries of what you can and can't do for your children, parents, or other relatives, and how to plan better with your spouse or partner. Because more and more Boomers want to work after retirement, we have devoted **Chapter 4: Reinventing Into New Work** to the subject of making money after retirement.

Here are our five ways to make your money last:

1. **Save more.**
2. **Keep making income.**
3. **Invest wisely and be diversified.**
4. **Have rental income and choose wisely where you live.**
5. **Cut back on expenses.**

Save More

This is what all financial planners say to us and certainly how our parents prepared for retirement, but it is not so simple in these economic times. For many, real income has fallen behind inflation and productivity and left little savings. The middle class has shrunk in terms of median income and buying power, and middle-class prosperity has been the foundation of the American life for the past 60 years. Our savings are diminished, or have disappeared in many cases, and we feel as though we are starting over at 50, 60, or 70. In fact, many of us are.

John had been a successful insurance executive and started his own recruiting business right before the recession hit. He also went through a divorce and had to pay for two households and alimony. Unfortunately, he had invested most of his retirement savings and lost almost everything he had. He had to start over at age 65 and is still struggling to bring back his business and recoup his savings. Current demands for his daughter's healthcare and educational expenses keep him constantly on the edge.

It is a sad story, but more common than you think. During the recession, the NFCC agencies saw a huge number of clients from the formerly upper and upper middle classes who had lost their savings or homes due to health issues or job loss. Many in the United States are just beginning to get a secure foothold back, and saving for retirement can be very tough. It comes down to finding more creative and innovative approaches to replenishing our savings. Here are some ways to save more:

* **Put any tax returns, inheritances, bonuses, and unexpected windfalls into retirement savings** and live on your income only.

* **Have a percentage taken out of your paycheck automatically** so if you don't see it, you don't spend it.

* **Maximize contributions to 401(k)s and IRAs, especially if matched by your company,** because otherwise you are leaving money on the table.

* **Make the extra contributions to 401(k)s and IRAs allowed for people over the age of 50**—a way to make up for lost time.

* **Go to a cash basis for expenditures** and save all extra cash at the end of a week from your allocated budget.

* **Cut out a bad habit** such as cigarettes or soft drinks and put the money into retirement savings. You will be amazed at what you save at $6 to $10 a pack, and you will be healthier for the future.

* **Get a part-time job and put it all into savings,** again living off of income only, even if it means you are working two jobs.

* **Sell assets you don't need and put into retirement savings**—assets like a third car or the boat, jewelry, or extra TVs.

* **Learn to barter** for goods and services.

* **Manage credit cards to zero balances** to avoid paying interest and fees.

* **Consider delaying your Social Security payments to age 70 to maximize the benefit** you will receive on a permanent basis, especially if you are a woman and are likely to live longer, but do be sure to talk to Social Security about whether you could receive special spousal benefits before age 70.

Keep Making Income

Because we expect to live longer than our parents and be in better health, we also may plan to work longer, especially if we have more control over what we do and can take time off. And many of us have no choice but to keep working to shore up our savings. However, many firms want to move older employees out and will not offer opportunities to stay or do part-time work. And there is still age discrimination. Americans 50-plus were hit the hardest with the recession.

The good news is that a growing number of businesses have a "welcome sign" for older workers. Part of this is explained by demographics because there are more Boomers in the age cohorts, but attitudes are also changing on the part of employers, who are recognizing that older adults bring skills and experience to the table that can help productivity and profitability. Some countries, such as Ireland, are already creating, and implementing, new policies targeted at Boomers, including retraining them for new careers. It is called the Ageing Well Network, and there is a Website for it in the Appendix.

A *Wall Street Journal* article by Andrea Coombes in October 2012 identifies four sectors that are good for older employees: education, financial services, healthcare, and professional services and knowledge workers. In these fields, experience and wisdom are valued and the age barriers and biases are less common. However, Coombes mentions that the three places where older employees stumble are in demanding high salaries and compensation (as they had before in their careers), being overconfident in their abilities and experience, and being less flexible in working styles or schedules.

> *Some people, such as Mary, leave a stressful career and position and just want to do a job that requires time and attention while at work, but no stress or take-home worries. That is why she now works three days a week at Target and loves it. Working for a retail store may give you more flexibility, as well as discounts on food, clothing, or other items, and allow you to enjoy meeting people and bringing in extra income, without the high-stress factor.*

The next chapter goes into this topic in detail, but here are a few ideas for leveraging your current work:

* **Stay on longer at your current position** at least for a few more years and avoid taking Social Security or drawing down on savings.

* **Work part-time at your current place of employment** or at a competitor. Negotiate this before you say you want to retire.

* **Become a consultant or "contract worker" in your field** and leverage your business contacts.

* **Start your own business** or buy into a franchise.

* **Leverage a hobby into a part-time job,** such as catering.

Invest Wisely and Be Diversified

Any good investment advisor or financial planner will tell you to diversify in your investment holdings, such as stocks, bonds, ETFs (exchange traded funds), and REITs (real estate investment trusts). The most important issue, in thinking about investments, is to understand the relationship among the variables of risk, return, savings, and consumption in achieving your goals. Each individual must understand his or her tolerance for risk. If an investment does not produce the desired return, then savings and consumption must be adjusted.

To get a good understanding of the amount of risk right for you, you may need to talk to professionals. There are a wide variety of types of financial advice professionals out there, so it can be confusing. First understand how they make their money—by selling you products and services or taking a fee. Just as you diversify your investments, you need to diversify your advice. For example, many investment firms will incentivize you to put all of your liquid assets with them to invest rather than using several investment firms. Usually there is a lower percentage fee if you hit certain levels of investments. (Depending on the level of your assets and whom you choose to manage your money, some CFAs/CFPs charge fees and others receive compensation via the investment companies they place assets in.)

Yet it is just as risky to use only one firm for your investments as it is to invest only in stocks or ETFs. Although there are some protections if the retirement and pension funds are impacted by a firm going bankrupt, just ask someone who invested most, or all, of their money with Bernie Madoff how it impacted their life.

Your financial inventory should include salaries, Social Security, real estate, pensions, inheritances, physical assets, insurance, antiques and collectibles, cars, savings and investment accounts, money people owe you, student loans, mortgage debt, and other debt and cash on hand. When you look at your total net worth (assets minus liabilities) it should be from a comprehensive perspective.

Then look for diversification. Are you too heavy in real estate? Do you have pensions and Social Security coming, and have you figured that value into the number you need to save for retirement? Did you inherit gold coins, art, other antiques or collectibles that may have value?

As our grandparents might have told us, "Don't put all your money in one pot." And don't overinvest in the company you work for. Many people who worked for Enron, Lehman Brothers, Polaroid, and other companies that went bankrupt or lost stock value lost their jobs, as well as their life savings and pensions. "Diversify, diversify, diversify" needs to be your mantra.

In the same vein, research and interview several financial or investment advisors and companies and compare how they each do versus the fees they charge.

We do not claim to be investment advisors or financial planners and urge you to find ones that you trust. But here are some pieces of advice we have gleaned as we have done our research:

* **Start by having a complete financial picture** of what you have and what you think you need.

* **Talk to a number of financial planners and investment advisors** and understand their fee structures. If they have incentives to steer your investments into their own company's investments, look for other alternatives.

* **Keep your money in at least two or three different firms,** plus Social Security and pension.

* **Review your financial situation at least once a year** comprehensively, and do it with your spouse, partner, and children.

* **Understand that if you need growth, you will need to be more in equities,** for a while.

* **Always have a "safety net" or "rainy day stash of money"** of at least six months to a year to get you through difficult times.

* **Use a money manager** if you do not like to pay day-to-day attention to your investments, but still stay on top of your managers.

* **Go to classes at local universities or colleges or online** to learn more about financial literacy and investments. Know that classes given by investment firms or banks may be marketing tools and not unbiased.

* **If you are in debt or underwater with your mortgage, go to the nearest NFCC agency** for help to get back on your financial feet.

* **Diversify, diversify, diversify.**

Have Rental Income and Choose Wisely Where You Live

This idea of having diversified sources of income when you plan the next chapter of your life should include a good discussion on housing. Even though you love your house and where you live, it is important to think about the cost of where you live versus other locales, the value and size of house you own or apartment you rent, and the needs you have as your family changes. For example, in most locales, homeowners near really good public schools pay more in real estate taxes. Is there another neighborhood that is desirable, but has lower taxes, once your children are grown?

Too often, people stay in their homes without understanding the financial implications of their decisions. That is not to say you are going to have to move, but it is important to understand the house as an asset, rather than just a place to live.

A recent *Wall Street Journal* report on retirement included a study of pre-retirees on whether they planned to move in retirement. The number one reason for those who planned to move (42 percent of the respondents planned to move) was cost of living (81 percent). Second was access to preferred healthcare programs (66 percent), and third was cultural activities (61 percent). Being close to children, grandchildren, or parents ranged in the 30- to 40-percent area. More than 49 percent said they would move to a different state, and the top states were in the Southeast and West.

Go to *www.revolutionary-retirement.com* to take the quiz on Finding Your Best Place to Retire and see the list of Best Places to Retire. CNNMoney.com's survey in 2013 has many more Western locales pop up due to lower income taxes, cost of living, weather, and cultural activities.

Renting all, or part, of your house is another option. This is especially attractive if you live in a city or college or university community or a travel destination. Consider buying and maintaining some rental properties near your hometown. Renting a home is an increasingly desirable option for many, and you may have the ability to rent your home out to others and live in an apartment for a period of time or take a vacation.

> *Mary rents her house in the Berkshires during high season and moves in with her daughter in the area. She saves enough to maintain her house throughout the year and have a little left over for her own vacation travel!*

There are rental agencies that can handle this for you, as well as Websites to list your house, such as *www.VRBO.com*. The Appendix lists many of those sites plus sites for home exchange, like *www.homeaway.com*

and *www.homeexchange.com.* You can also rent your apartment through groups like Airbnb, or might even consider having a bed and breakfast in your home, if zoning allows. In Austin, many people rent out their homes and apartments during South by Southwest, and the city allows it for that one week.

Mortgages

In the past many people had the goal of paying off their mortgage, if they had one, before they retired. But today, there are many reasons still to carry a mortgage. A better use of your extra money might be in investments. The current interest rates are low, and by refinancing, you may have a very reasonable mortgage rate. You may also have a house with a mortgage that is "underwater" and will have to carry the house until real estate prices improve further. Downsizing may also bring a smaller mortgage. There is no one answer...but what is right for you.

There are a few smart strategies for managing your mortgage for retirement:

* **Refinance to a lower interest rate** while we are at low levels.

* **Refinance to shorten your loan's time frame.**

* **Make a lump-sum payment** to reduce the interest you pay, as well as the length of the loan.

* **Switch to biweekly payments,** which will also reduce interest paid over the life of the loan.

* **Round up your payment each month,** even if only from $975 to $1,000, to make a big difference in what you owe in interest.

If you are tempted to look at a reverse mortgage on your house that promises to pay you an annuity for as long as you live there, please be very careful with this option. Talk to others who have done it. For many people it is not a good investment, and the fees to do it and the loss of the asset to your heirs may be detrimental to your financial well-being. Be sure to have both of your names on the agreement. In some states, if both names are not on the original documentation, the property reverts to the lender and the surviving person may have to move out of the house. There also are implications for those in your will/estate, as they will have the option of purchasing the property. This needs to be understood, as it often comes as a surprise that the heirs will need to pay for the house or take out another mortgage. If you do consider a reverse mortgage, please go to a trained NFCC professional or a trusted non-bank financial advisor to discuss all the implications. In fact, it is now mandatory for people who seek reverse mortgages to receive counseling first.

Housing by Decade

Think about housing in terms of decades. What you need now to house your "boomerang" single kids or families with grandchildren will change as the grandchildren grow older and your need for a big house diminishes. On the other hand, many people are adding rooms on to their houses to care for aging relatives. But for how long? And larger houses take more maintenance and renovation costs. Do you really need that when you are in your 80s or 90s?

> *One of the best revelations Angela got from talking to her accountant was that the house she now has, which does have room for many family members and friends and requires quite a bit of upkeep, will not be what she wants when she is in her 80s. She will be traveling to see the nieces and nephews in their homes and may want the simplicity of a smaller home or apartment. She will be ready to give up the larger house, and that asset will contribute to her retirement funds for her 80s and 90s, if she is lucky enough to live that long.*

Our desires and needs will change by decade, and we should plan accordingly. There are some innovative solutions emerging in areas like San Francisco and Boston, where aging people are forming neighborhood associations that have many of the benefits of assisted living. They have arranged for someone to provide meals, do maintenance on houses, provide home healthcare, and other services to homeowners in the neighborhood that allow them to stay in their homes and apartments.

In other areas of the country, people are building or moving into multigenerational housing with their relatives or friends or creating compounds where friends live together. The old "commune" concept of the Sixties just might be revived for the Boomers, albeit in a different manner.

Cut Back on Expenses

Cutting back on expenses does not have to be a painful experience. It is a matter of having a different perspective, valuing time and experiences over material things, and tailoring your lifestyle to fit your dreams. It is also about resetting expectations.

You can have a rich life without spending that much money.

There are many options before you to fund what you want to do. It is a matter of balance between income generation and expense cutting. Here are a number of ways to cut expenses:

* **See your local Websites for fun and inexpensive things to do** in your hometown, such as going to free concerts and Sundays at the museum.

* **Downsize, rent, or trade your home** to live in a different locale or save money on vacations or share housing with others.

* **Get health insurance through a health exchange or group or association that lowers your cost of supplemental insurance.**

* **Cook at home more often** and splurge on lunch out when prices are lower.

* **Barter for goods and services** with skills or assets you have.

* **Put boundaries** on giving to your children.

* **Stay healthy.** Practice preventive measures that will save you costs in the long run.

* **Join group "buying clubs"** to get better prices on things.

* **Visit yard sales,** discount stores, and other sources of reduced-priced goods.

* **Take public transportation or use shared cars** and get rid of one, or all, of your cars.

* **Do shared meals** with friends and cut back on cooking as well as food costs by buying in bulk.

* **Go through your utility and energy costs** and find ways to cut them through decreased use or more energy-efficient products.

* **Frequent sports events and other recreational activities that have specials** or are lower cost.

* **Use your AARP and senior discounts** for movies, plays, transportation and other things. Don't be too proud!

Balancing Your Role as the "Sandwich Generation"

Boomerang Kids

We cannot tell you how many of our friends and relatives are dealing with launching their children, living with "boomerang children," and subsidizing their kids through their 30s and 40s. Remember when we graduated from school or college and could not wait to have our own place, make our own money, and not ask our parents for things? The Boomers, for the most part, were self-sufficient and would have dreaded having to ask for help. It was a passage of adulthood to earn your own way.

That's not to say that parents didn't help with graduate school or with the down payment on a first house, if they had the means, but today many young adults are asking for rental subsidies, moving home to save on housing and food costs, or asking parents to buy a home for them. In fact, 39 percent of young adults say they are living with their parents now or have moved back temporarily. And that is impacting their parents' savings.

Why is this happening? You can blame the rising costs of living, the rising student loans, the lack of good-paying jobs, and the need for people to live in a safe place. However, it is also partly the Boomers' fault for creating an environment where the children expect a certain lifestyle, and for their parents to fund it.

To launch your children, teaching them financial savvy and budgeting capabilities will go a long way toward helping you plan your next chapter. But you also need to set boundaries on what they can expect from you. The greatest gift we can give our children beyond love and a good education is the wherewithal to take care of themselves. It is important for their self-esteem and ability to navigate the world, and it is important for them to understand, and respect, your boundaries. Make sure your kids have a firm grasp of budgeting, financial planning, and saving for retirement themselves. Tell them the power of compounding (growth of assets that are left untouched) and the value of investing even a little, starting early. Open Roth IRAs (low cost and tax free) for them. Teach them to save for their future.

Mike and Norinne are so proud of their three daughters, now married and in their 30s, because they have never come back to them for money. They taught them well about saving for the future, having a good education to get a good job, and how to manage their money frugally, even when they were teenagers. The young women take pride in the fact they are independent. Mike and Norinne did set up a trust for each of the daughters to go to them when they pass away, but it is set up for limited access and emergencies only today. Financial literacy at an early age paid off!

Caring for Elderly Parents

Likewise, you may be responsible for caring for elderly parents or relatives, and you need to know what you can and cannot do, as well as what services are available to help you. Hopefully, your parents have the resources to take care of themselves, even if in a nursing home. But the reality is more likely that you will have to help in some way. It is a very difficult and emotional thing to go through—not only switching roles to where you are the "parent," but seeing your parents and relatives decline and no longer able to care for themselves. Put financial pressures on top of that, and you have a very challenging future.

Laura's mother became more fragile, requiring around-the-clock nursing. Laura could no longer afford the living arrangement for her mother (they had already gone through her mother's assets), and her mother didn't understand that. Working with her siblings, the nursing home, her mother's doctor, and a healthcare consultant, they were able to move her mother to a nursing home in a single room with around-the-clock care, and her mother became eligible for Medicaid. It was a traumatic experience for everyone, but, with the help of a team of emotional and medical care consultants, they were able to make the change.

Many Baby Boomers are going to come to this point of sacrifice, and they will need to protect their own retirement funds.

Start by talking to your parents and relatives now about how they want to deal with future health and living situations, especially in light of the financial resources available. Make sure they have wills, living wills, and health and financial powers of attorney. Make sure they have listed all their assets and account information, and that you will be able to find everything or access it. Start focusing on the place that they currently live. Is it adaptable to aging needs such as having a single floor plan, handrails in bathrooms, safe flooring? Is their home in a safe area? Are there any changes, especially financial, they can make now in preparation for the future?

Do your parents or relatives have long-term care insurance or other resources to help them pay for a nursing home, healthcare workers in the home, and the rising healthcare costs that come with age? Do you? It is best to buy long-term care when you are in your 50s or early 60s, as it gets more expensive as you get older. Most experts say that the majority of healthcare costs come in the last six months of a person's life. Most people prefer to stay at home and receive healthcare services there, especially if terminally ill. Managing those costs must be part of your and your parent's retirement plans.

And when you are doing this, think about what you can do to help your children when they come to this point with you! You will read more about these topics in **Chapter 7: Renegotiating Life at Home** and **Chapter 8: Most Important of All: Your Health.**

Another consideration in creating a budget is pets. Pets are so much a part of our families. Often, at the same time we are dealing with elderly parents and their health issues, we are dealing with aging and dying of beloved pets acquired when the kids were young. Average expenditure over the lifetime of a domestic pet, like a dog, is $2,000–6,000 (and can be much higher), and much of that is on health-related issues as the pet ages. There is pet insurance, but it does not cover many expenses. During the recession, many animals were turned in to rescue centers, as people were not able to afford to feed and keep them.

Investing in Yourself

At the start of this chapter, we talked about the bucket of assets you have and that the most important one is *you*. Yes, *you* are more important than savings. Yes, *you,* because you are the navigator of your future. Investing in yourself is the single best way you can ensure that you will realize your dreams. It means putting your dreams first and making sure you have the right resources to achieve them. So what does that mean? Following are some ways that you can be sure you have made yourself not only relevant, but needed by your employer, clients, partners, family, friends, and potential career colleagues.

Keep Up With Technology

You probably already know how to use a computer, but do you know how to use all the functions? Do you have a tablet or smartphone and are you able to navigate it to the fullest? Do you text as well as e-mail? Do you know how to download apps, take pictures and videos, and use multiple types of software? Don't despair! Your own Team of Experts from grandkids to the Geek Squad to online resources can help. Think of it as learning a new culture or language and explore away! Whether you actually like using the stuff or hate it, it is important to understand what is available, what your kids and grandkids are using, and how it is impacting society. We view this skill set as one of the most important to acquire and maintain because it is a "given expectation" with employers that you understand and use technology. If you can't, it may make you unemployable.

Marketing Yourself

It's all about the contacts! You will need them for full- or part-time work, for your fund-raising for charities, to get onto non-profit and corporate boards, to market your first book or start that catering business! When you leave work, be sure to bring your contacts and mailing lists with you. Continue to collect business cards and to network where you can. Get directories from your university, church, and social groups to continue to grow your contact list. Understand how to use social media, such as Facebook, Twitter, Pinterest, Instagram, and LinkedIn. Though you might not like to use social media or think it is a waste of time, it is what your kids, grandkids, colleagues, and employers are using. The senior vice president of human resources of a global pharmaceutical firm told us that if someone doesn't have a LinkedIn profile and submits a resume on paper, they think he is not a good candidate, because he's not up with technology.

To market yourself, you need to continually update your LinkedIn profile, resume and bio. Have it ready to send for a potential board position, part-time or full-time opportunity, a Website that lists consultants, or to the magazine that publishes your article. Whatever the purpose, you need to keep it current and be on LinkedIn.

Speaking at industry events and doing webinars is another way for your name to get out there and establish your knowledge base. Although you may not get paid for speaking, it is a way to meet new people, prospective employers or clients, and colleagues who might recommend you for a job or board. Ask your trade association for an opportunity to be on a panel at an upcoming meeting, send in proposals for topics, ask your current employer for opportunities and look at what community colleges and other local organizations are doing. Go speak to a class at a university. These events are wonderful networking opportunities as well.

Stay active, involved, and relevant, and continue to network all your life, if not to help you, then to help others that you mentor. Read the book *Stiletto Network* to understand how important networking with peers can be at all ages of life.

Top-10 Must Do's

Let us leave you with what we think are the top-10 must do's in planning your financial future and making your money last. Just remember: You have many options and even if you have not saved enough for retirement, there are myriad ways for you to live your dreams by altering your perspective. We hope this chapter has given you some tools to do that!

1. **Get your financial facts and "stuff" together.**
2. **Learn whom to trust,** and why, for financial advice.
3. **Prepare for the unexpected** and budget accordingly.
4. **Diversify, diversify, diversify.**
5. **Explore all the options** and recognize you have them.
6. **Plan by the decade** because your needs will change.

7. **See yourself as your biggest asset and invest in yourself.**

8. **Set boundaries** with children and relatives.

9. **Plan for higher healthcare costs** and health issues.

10. **Communicate and coordinate** with your spouse or partner.

✎ Exercise 3-1: Getting Your Finances in Order

Ask yourself the following questions and put the answers in your journal to reflect on in the future:

❑ What are my fears about getting my finances in order?

❑ Am I impacting my retirement savings by subsidizing my children?

❑ Have my spouse/partner and I really talked about finances and budgets?

❑ How can I best invest in myself to stay relevant and employable, if need be?

❑ What are three things I can do this week to feel more at peace about money?

CHAPTER 4

Reinventing Into New Work

If you don't like the road you're walking, start paving another one.

—Dolly Parton

Many Baby Boomers are leaving their long-time jobs but fear their Social Security benefits and retirement nest eggs will prove to be too small, especially as they project better health and longevity. So they are plunging into full- and part-time work—from being a consultant to being a sales clerk. Others are stepping down from their careers but then concluding, after a year or two, that they are bored and want to start their own businesses or go back to work in a new career. They were just not ready for retirement.

This chapter is about reinventing into new work—that is, finding opportunities and avenues that use your skills and passions so you can continue to earn money and be fulfilled beyond your already-interesting activities. You can design a new work life on your own terms—something different and exciting and more flexible than your full-time career. It may be just as intense if you are pursuing a passion, but it is a new chapter in a new context.

Yes, There Are Jobs

Assuming a continued return to healthy economic growth and no change in immigration or labor force participation rates, Barry Bluestone, dean of the School of Public Policy and Urban Affairs at Northeastern University, predicted in 2013 that within the next eight years there could be at least five million potential job vacancies in the United States, nearly half of them (2.4 million) social sector jobs in education, healthcare, government, and nonprofit organizations. The resulting loss in total output if the jobs aren't filled could limit the growth of needed services and cost the economy as much as $3 trillion over the five-year period beginning in 2018.

"If the baby boom generation retires from the labor force at the same rate and age as current older workers, the baby bust generation that follows will likely be too small to fill many of the projected new jobs," states Bluestone's report, *After the Recovery: Help Needed—The Coming Labor Shortage and How People in Encore Careers Can Help Solve It.*

The good news for us Baby Boomers is that there will be lots of options, both part-time and full-time, for making money after retiring from our previous careers. The new job could be in the same field or a different one, just as intense or less intense.

Tony retired from an executive position at the U.S. Postal Service. Within a few months, he had gone to work at a major transit enterprise where his experience and skills were greatly appreciated.

Many retailers have created a deliberate strategy for hiring older employees. The benefit to retailers is that they get mature, reliable workers. We, in turn, get flexibility with choosing our hours of work and often get a nice retail discount.

Zanna, a former Ringling Brothers and Barnum & Bailey Circus public relations executive, enjoyed retirement from her stressful job at first. She and her husband moved from the East Coast to the Northwest, where she enjoyed hiking in the gorgeous Pacific Northwest, studying French, and traveling with her husband. But then her husband passed away. After a period of mourning, she tried to fill the void by enrolling in an immersion language course in France. She enjoyed it but knew it was still just an escape from being home alone. Knowing she needed to get out of the house, she went in search of a stress-free job. She loved to cook, so approaching the retail cookware shop Williams-Sonoma was a no brainer. She got the job and they got a great employee. Fast-forward a couple of years, and she is remarried—to a widower she met at the store.

Want to work from home? Angie is funding her retirement by living on a couple's property looking after their house when they are not there. Michel, formerly a technology employee, continues to work part-time as a freelance programmer from his home.

Carol promotes herself as a personal assistant. She's known in her neighborhood as the cheerful person who does work to make others' lives less hectic. She files, sorts closets, runs errands, does the grocery shopping, or whatever.

Perhaps you have a love of animals and might want to house-sit for a cat or other animal while the owners are away. Being a dog walker allows you to choose your own hours of work, brings in some money, and gets you outdoors and exercising at the same time. Dan makes $100 a day as a combination house and pet sitter in Colorado, plus he gets to enjoy living in different towns and neighborhoods.

Staying Professional

We talked in **Chapter 3: Making Your Money Last** about *you* as one of your key assets. Depending on your current career or career interests in the future, you may feel you need to find ways to develop or maintain your professional skills in a given field. There are certifications for positions such as Certified Financial Planner or Certified Information Security Professional. There are courses to take for a degree or certification and professional updating. Many lawyers, accountants, planners, plumbers, electricians, and other professionals have local, state, and federal requirements for continued education and certification.

And, it is never too late to go back to school! There are many stories of 60-, 70-, and 80-year-olds going back for classes or degrees, and colleges and universities are gearing up for this. Adult education is booming, and community colleges, online courses, alma maters, and others are vying for the adult student, often at reduced tuition. Seeing mature adults in classes is par for the course.

Russ was an AT&T executive until he retired. He then rebooted and went to divinity school. Upon graduation, he became a Unitarian minister. For several years, he happily led a church, then retired again. Shortly after, a friend asked him to serve while his assistant minister was away on sabbatical. Then came another such request, and another, and another. Russ is working part-time in his current ministerial position and enjoying a rich and balanced life, including time with his wife and grown children. His retirement chapter thus far has been a very fulfilling second career and life for him.

People who are interested in changing careers often opt to intern in a new career area for free, such as learning to be a chef, building a piece of furniture, working as a legal assistant or at a nonprofit. Many colleges help adults find internship opportunities through the adult education and extension programs.

Speaking a foreign language (and keeping it current) is another great skill that is needed at any age. There are opportunities to teach, translate, write, speak, and advise companies that target a certain language market. Having the cultural knowledge as well as the language speaking skill is even better. Many companies are starting to hire cultural anthropologists to try to better understand how to create and market new products and services to non-English speaking people. Needless to say, many nonprofits that are involved in social and community issues need this skill as well.

Special Resources

Two great organizations we encourage you to become familiar with are Encore.org and AARP. Encore.org began as Civic Ventures in 1997, founded by social entrepreneur Marc Freedman to transform the aging of America into a powerful source of individual and social renewal. In 2012, Civic Ventures became known as Encore.org. The organization's focus is to draw Boomers to encore careers that provide personal fulfillment doing paid work. In doing so, a windfall of talent can be put to work to help solve the most challenging social problems of our time, including poverty, hunger, the environment, education, and healthcare.

Encore.org manages an inventive program portfolio, including fellowships and prizes. The organization publishes original research that illuminates society's need for encore talent and the desire among Boomers to start encore careers.

You may know of AARP, but may not be familiar with the breadth of services it offers. It is a nonprofit, nonpartisan membership organization for people age 50 and over, dedicated to enhancing the quality of life for all as we age.

AARP has a robust Website (*www.aarp.org*) that is a great resource for paid and unpaid work. Its Life Reimagined for Work section (*www.lifereimagined.org*) helps experienced professionals find jobs, manage their careers, start businesses, and explore options. It has a job-search section, search tips, interactive discussion groups, and all sorts of informative articles, including some on how to start your own business.

Teaching

You've read stories of people going back to school for certifications. How about considering teaching itself? Many of us wanted to be teachers when we were in our younger stages but thought it simply didn't pay enough. Others of us have discovered that the parts of work that gives us the most joy are mentoring others and imparting information. There is no nobler career in life than helping to mold our next generation; we need good teachers everywhere. Teaching English as a Second Language, for example, does not require a teaching degree. At universities, community colleges, and business schools, you do not have to have a teaching degree to teach courses as a retired executive. Adjunct work does not have huge financial returns, but it is certainly stimulating, is rewarding, and keeps using a skill that you have honed for years.

Nancy is an adjunct professor, using her government and nonprofit national security experience to teach a graduate course. Many of her colleagues in Washington, DC, do the same.

When Eileen and Cono stopped working full time, they both guest lectured at the University of Bologna, while living in that city for two months. As a result, they were offered positions teaching a seminar course the next year.

Some of you might want to consider going back to school to get a teaching degree for teaching from elementary to high school.

Nick retired as a bond salesman and now teaches autistic children. He went to school at night and on the weekends, timing graduation with his retirement from the world of finance. Today, he loves his work and says he is happier than he has ever been.

Barter

Bartering is a great way to swap your services to receive something in return that you would have had to pay for otherwise. You can barter skills such as design, legal services, childcare, programming, tax preparation or web development, home improvement, life or sports coaching, teaching in person or via teleclasses, and translation, if you are fluent in a foreign language. Jim traded writing a resume for his neighbor in exchange for a few good dinners. Sarah traded yoga sessions for house repairs. Websites such as *www.imsbarter.com* and *www.swapright.com* help set up barter trade exchanges. In Timebank, you put your service hours into a bank and then take out services rendered by another.

Joyce, who was an experienced and happy user of Timebank services, reported, "I have enlisted the skills of a dentist for cleanings and fillings, a home maintenance person, a massage therapist, and an astrologer. My contributions have been in planning events for Timebank. My experience has been that people give more freely and provide superior services when money is not exchanged. It feels like the work is coming from the heart."

Bartering is also a great way to start as a self-employed service provider, especially in a difficult economy, when you are faced with clients who need your services and want to hire you, but are unable to pay you in cash at the moment. You can set a price for your offerings and you can work out a plan with the client to compensate you with goods or service of equal value to the cash price you set. We also spoke to several people who said that allowing people to become familiar with their services via barter led to paid work after a period of time.

Starting a New Business

Ever dreamed of starting your own business? Now just might be the time. The sky is the limit for new business ideas. But not all new businesses require major funding or investment capital. Many successful businesses start out of one's home with a small investment. Perhaps you make jewelry or pottery, or restore toy antique trains that you can sell out of your home. There's catering and all sorts of other services. Consulting, starting an errand-running service, planning parties, setting up a computer help service, creating a childcare service—these are a few of the businesses you can start for less than $5,000.

> *Robin has been able to save for her daughter's education just by buying and selling things on eBay. She often goes to estate and yard sales and, because she has a good eye and knows value, has made some great investments. She sells for others and takes a commission. She is currently working at a pawn store in the Southwest to be able to find good American Indian jewelry, pots, and baskets, which she turns around and sells.*

We encourage you to return to the visualization exercise in **Chapter 2: Planning and Designing Your Reinvention.** Let your mind wander, then write down in your journal lots of ideas, no matter how far out you may think they are. Test them against your interest and abilities, and then winnow them down.

You can go to your local community college or business school to take a course on how to start and run a small business. Read books and talk to small business owners in your areas of interest. Perhaps work for them as a volunteer or intern to learn the business.

When considering a new business idea, we strongly suggest exploring mini-trials or internships. Talk to lots of people who have set up their own businesses to understand the pros and cons. Then find someone in a similar field, but not a direct competitor, whom you might approach to ask if you can intern with him or her. And if not as an intern, then try to shadow him or her at work for a week or two.

Also, be careful what you ask for.

Dave and his wife had always wanted to start a bed and break-fast. They bought a charming old farmhouse in the Berkshires and, with her keen eye to decorating and collecting antiques, they created the most welcoming environment. At first they loved cooking and meeting people from all over the world, but after a year or so the work simply became overwhelming, and they sold the inn.

Instead of starting a business that stems from one of your ideas, you may prefer franchising an existing business.

Charlie, upon his retirement from the computer industry, moved from northern winters to Florida, where he bought the franchise for a couple of fast food restaurants. They grew, and he bought a couple more. This type of business provided the money he desired for his next phase of life and provided him the flexibility to do many of the other things he and his wife wanted to do during retirement.

The U.S. Small Business Administration (SBA) has many programs in every region to help entrepreneurs as well as a wonderful cadre of volunteer resources in SCORE, the organization of retired executives. The SBA Website (*www.sba.gov*) has a wealth of information including how to create a business plan, choosing your business structure, how to register it and obtain licenses, business law, filing and paying taxes, hiring, retaining employees, and financing your business. Once you're up and running, there are informative articles on leading your business, growing it, and even getting out.

We recommend educating yourself with basic information before hiring a lawyer, but you probably should use a lawyer if you are going to incorporate. Become familiar with legal requirements from sales taxes to bookkeeping. Make sure to get a separate business bank account and phone line or cell number. You can start by setting up a simple Website so people can find you, which may require another expert. Business cards are available quickly and inexpensively at Websites like VistaPrint.com and Zazzle.com.

Regarding financing, the SBA provides a number of financial assistance programs for small businesses. They guide you through identifying loans and preparing your loan application and identifying funding sources, such as government grants, venture capital, and other assistance.

The Boomers as a Market

One way to think about opportunities to make your money last as a Baby Boomer is to think about yourself and your age cohort as a market for which you can create new products and services. The 50-plus population in the United States is the third-largest economy in the world, beaten only by the U.S. economy as a whole and China. There are more than 100 million people who generate $7 trillion a year in goods and services. Every year, their buying power and numbers expand. Here are some of the trends and product ideas from the March 2011 *AARP Bulletin* that you might explore, with a full list in the article:

* **Looking great.** The Boomers all want to look younger and fit, and the market for anti-aging products, nutritional supplements, cosmetics, and other related products is booming. Boomers like teams of advisors, such as Pilates instructors, massage therapists, personal trainers, nutritionists. Spas are a $12.3B a year industry. Health club membership is rapidly growing for the 55+ age group.

* **Staying wired.** Boomers are 41 percent of Apple computer buyers today. SeniorNet is a national nonprofit that helps seniors learn how to use computers and the Internet. The Geek Squad has 20,000 technicians that do house calls 24/7.

* **Going green.** Eighty percent of Boomers view themselves as "green"; 75 percent of Boomers say they recycle.

* **Driving housing.** As Boomers add millions of people to the senior population, demands for affordable, accessible housing will increase.

Consulting

Before you retired, you had a skill that obviously your company or organization valued. So why wouldn't someone else? Starting a consulting business is one way to draw upon your expertise and creatively make use of problem-solving skills. You can choose how much time you want to work and which days. It gives you flexibility, and it can be lucrative.

Lynn retired after working 39 years for IBM. After a while, she said to herself, "I can't play golf all the time, and I have to use my brain." Lynn was losing some of her oomph and self-confidence when a friend suggested she attend one of our Reboot Your Life workshops. After a couple of days together and hearing her story, we and other participants suggested, "Why not consider consulting?" Shortly afterward, Lynn was speaking with an old friend who informed her that IBM was bringing back retirees part-time. Why? Retirees know the company, the people, the processes—there's no training needed. Lynn called us with such excitement in her voice as she shared that she had been hired as a consultant/contractor. She helps IBM manage and integrate the contracts of newly acquired companies. "Project management is one of my strengths. I work from home or I take my computer and can travel anywhere. It's a win-win for everyone, including my golf game. I love it. I choose which projects and at which time. I can take it or leave it. I never had confidence before to choose projects. I was afraid if I didn't do one, the work would shrivel up."

If you are considering consulting, talk to friends who have done so. Don't know anyone? Not to worry. Think about the concept of six degrees of separation—who you know and who they know. Call friends and ask if they know anyone. Usually they do, and we find that if approached properly, even strangers will give you time and share insights and contacts. See our Website for tips on networking.

If you are ready to set up a consulting business, consider partnering with another firm while building your own business. You will need to think about how to differentiate your services. Many say they are in "strategic consulting." What does that mean? It's difficult for friends to refer you to others if they do not easily understand what you do, if everyone sounds the same. Do you work in a specific industry or with a specific functional skill? What makes you different?

Staying involved in your professional associations with individual memberships is a wonderful way to meet people, find consulting opportunities, and keep up with the issues and technology facing your field. Many associations have "retired rates" or opportunities to volunteer in exchange for attending the meetings. Most trade associations are looking for good articles and/or blogs. Start your own Website and blog on issues in your particular field of expertise!

Lots of other advice is available on how to start a consulting business. Talk to your lawyer or accountant on whether to incorporate. You can also form a company online at LegalZoom (*www.legalzoom.com*). One example of online help can be found at www.rac-tqi.com. If you prefer books, there's *The Everything Start Your Own Consulting Business* or *Start Your Own Consulting Business*. Then there are startup books that are field-specific. There's even a startup book on wedding consulting.

Interim Management

Should you continue to want to work for a short period of time or longer, then interim management may be just the thing for you.

You were an expert in your work; why not lend your skills and experience to helping another company or organization? One usually hears about interim CEO positions, but there are also organizations that specialize in placing interim CFOs or CIOs or CMOs (chief marketing officers) or other key management positions. You can find opportunities listed by geography, industry, or functional expertise, such as chief information security officer. Look in both the for-profit and nonprofit worlds.

Sharon, instead of retiring, became an early pioneer in this concept when she founded WAHVE (Work at Home for Vintage Employees). The company offers a domestic remote staffing solution for insurance agents and brokers. Sharon believes in capturing the power of Baby Boomers, people in the industry with 25–30 years' experience who have retired. These interim employees know they want or need to continue working, but they want flexibility and don't want to work from an office anymore. That's why they retired. WAHVE gives them the opportunity to work at home at a much lower cost for the companies. Today the technology exists to do so. Everyone wins. Agencies and insurance companies win because they save money and get amazing talent—someone with 20 or 30 years' experience—and the employee gets supplemental income while working from home remotely.

The Appendix lists Websites to help get you started if interim management is of interest to you.

A Portfolio Career

Many of us have a number of skills and interests but may not want a full-time job just focusing on one thing. Many people are taking into consideration all of their interests and talents and doing two, three, or even four different things that all tap into their interests and skills. Thinking about what we have already described, you can teach a day or two a week. You can write a blog or articles. You can consult on a per diem basis as needed, and you can work part-time at a bookstore or at places such as Costco or Target. You can even volunteer part of your time. The point is that now you are in charge and can formulate a plan that gives you flexibility, keeps you engaged in things you love, and provides you with an income—but just in a different way than you might have been used to in the past.

Investing in Others and in Ideas

Angel Investing

An angel investor is someone willing to invest in a company at its early stages of development in exchange for an ownership stake. Angels are considered one of the oldest sources of capital for startup entrepreneurs. Angels tend to invest both their funds and their expertise locally and like to play an active role in the development of the companies in which they invest. Whereas some people make investments independently, many have chosen to form groups to get a better deal flow, share the due diligence and administrative work, and improve their investing success by pooling their expertise and ideas. If you have the financial wherewithal and business experience, angel investing can be very rewarding. See *www.angelcapital-association.org* for a list of angel groups in the United States, Canada, and Mexico.

> *Upon retirement, Katherine chose to become an angel investor with Golden Seeds (www.goldenseeds.com). She enjoys the opportunity to meet other really smart businesspeople from all different industries and to stay current with innovation and young entrepreneurs. She took her time in joining, attended a few meetings as a guest, and asked lots of questions. She made her selection based*

upon their mission of investing in women-led businesses, the strong deal flow, and their very rigorous due diligence methodology.

Kevin combines angel investing with an academic program.

Kevin co-founded the first commercially successful software company in Idaho 40 years ago and is a former entrepreneurship professor and college president. At 62, he moved from running a company back to a university to work with entrepreneurs. Plus, he started doing angel investing and helped to raise three angel funds to support local entrepreneurs. Now in his later 60s, he founded and directs Venture College at Boise State University, which supports students as they attempt to launch businesses or nonprofit ventures while pursuing their education.

Another way to invest—often with very low levels of capital ($25 or less)—without formal investing organizations like angel groups is through organizations like Kickstarter. It is one of the top vehicles to offer the opportunity to lend money and invest in projects or businesses in which you are interested. The projects are wide and diverse from Cindy, a hairdresser in NYC who is producing a new salsa, to restoring the old Roxy Theatre in Philadelphia, to funding the first-ever 3D printing pen. In exchange for your money you may get early access to a nifty new product or a potential financial return. Another of our Kickstarter favorites is a project to create a film on how 10-year-olds view peace and the imperatives for peace.

If you like the idea of working as an angel investor, you might want to consider impact investing. Impact investments are investments made in companies, organizations, and funds with the intention to generate measurable social and environmental impact along with a financial return. As an investor, it's a way to avoid the tyranny of "either/or." You can make money and do good at the same time. Impact investors ask and answer the question *What kind of world do I want my money to create?*

Or if you want simply to invest in great nonprofit causes, maybe even one that you've created yourself, check out Indiegogo, Zidisha, or Kiva, which have a mission to connect people directly to clients. Kiva, for example, by leveraging the internet and a worldwide network of microfinance institutions, lets individuals make loans as small as $25. Since beginning in 2005 and as of August 2015, there were 1,336,669 Kiva lenders, who, working with 300 field partners have given $748,563,025 in loans in 83 countries.

Crowdsourcing

Crowdsourcing is the practice of outsourcing tasks to a broad, loosely defined external group of people. The term was first coined in 2006 by *Wired* magazine author Jeff Howe in an article titled "The Rise of Crowdsourcing." Howe suggested that crowdsourcing encouraged the best-qualified and most creative participants to join in on a project. You could be one of these subject matter expert participants or crowdworker.

As early as 1936, Toyota held a contest seeking a new logo design. The winning design, from more than 26,000 entries, remained the company's corporate logo until 1989. Today iStockPhoto allows amateur and professional photographers, illustrators, and videographers to upload their work and earn royalties when their images or videos are bought and downloaded.

In 2012, Lays ran a contest called "Do Us a Flavor" in which they asked people to create the newest potato chip flavor. People submitted their creative concoctions through a Facebook app on the Lays page. A judging panel comprised of chefs, foodies, flavor experts, and actress Eva Longoria narrowed down submissions to three flavors. Facebook fans then voted for one of these flavors. The winner received one million dollars (or 1 percent of the chips' net sales in 2013, whichever was more). For crowdsource sites looking for translating, editing, writing, data processing, design, marketing, video production, and other skills, see the Appendix.

For-Profit Board Service

Boards offer the opportunity to stay relevant and work with interesting people on interesting issues on a part-time basis while earning a nice compensation. In its 2011–2012 Directors Compensation Report, the National Association of Corporate Directors (NACD) found that median 2011 director pay ranged from approximately $96,000 (micro companies) to $230,000 (top 200 companies), usually with a mix of cash and equity.

But, if you are joining a board just for the money, you shouldn't do it. Instead, choose to serve on a board because you feel you have the skill set and knowledge that can help a particular company, have strong desire to contribute to its strategy and growth, and sense your contributions will be welcomed.

Joining a for-profit board is a serious commitment. Board and committee meeting attendance, conference calls, the enormous amount of reading and prep work, all take lots of time and hard work. If you are interested in the money only, you would be better off consulting in most cases. However, the income from a board acts as an annuity and can be figured into your income stream at least until age 72, when many boards have a mandatory stop for members.

As would be expected, although there are legal protections in place, there are also several personal liability risks that directors must consider—lawsuits, new guidelines for cyber security, more government investigations and enforcement, a new whistleblower program, and more. Sarbanes-Oxley legislation and the Dodd-Frank Act have added much more governance and oversight to boards. Before committing, ask the following questions about the board you're considering joining:

* Will your service make a difference?
* Is there a clear process for sharing information, and open lines of communication among the board, management, and constituents?
* Do you understand all of your roles and responsibilities?
* Is the board composition diverse?
* Is there any outstanding litigation that is worrisome?
* What kind of financial situation is the board facing?
* Is this an industry you know something about or have an interest in?
* What skill sets do you bring, such as knowledge of technology or financial audits?
* What is the reputation of the organization and the industry?
* Is this industry or company undergoing government scrutiny?
* Do you have the time bandwidth to be on a board? Most boards only allow you to be on two or three others.

Getting on a Board

Getting onto boards, especially your first one and ones you want, can be tricky. Most corporate boards are looking for sitting or former CEOs or executives with specialized expertise, such as financial audit knowledge, operations, technology, or risk management. Boards are also recognizing the importance of diversity, and more than 50 percent of current board openings are requesting to see qualified people of color and women. If you believe that you are qualified to serve on a board and have the interest, start by creating a profile. See our Website for a sample profile.

You probably have a stellar resume, but most likely it highlights your operational success. Create a board-specific resume and bio that focuses on the strategic side of your background and accomplishments. All the major search firms have recruiters who specialize in board searches, and you should get to know them. But getting on a board is still a "who knows who" game. More than 50 percent of board openings are filled without the use of a recruiting firm. And even when they are used, it is to vet people the board already knows and proposes. It is therefore important that you work your own personal network as well.

We recommend when interviewing with the company, where possible, to have several one-on-one interviews rather than a group one. The benefit to you is that you get to calibrate questions and answers from various perspectives. It's a way to get to understand more about the culture and how aligned everyone is. Also try to meet with members of the management team in addition to the CEO, members such as the CFO, general counsel, and a head of an operating unit. Questions that we recommend asking are listed on our Website.

Doing research on a company's history, performance, competitors, and so forth is the easy part of due diligence. Getting to know the culture and if you will fit and enjoy spending much of your time with this company are the reasons why the interviews and the questions you pose are key to a successful board match.

As you do your homework on companies, also become familiar with organizations and media dedicated to the board world. See the Appendix for more information.

We are frequently asked if serving on a not-for-profit board helps one in obtaining a public board position. The big recruiters who specialize in board placements would tell you no. Whereas being on a nonprofit board may not specifically get you on a board, it is our opinion that you gain many other benefits. Most nonprofits, at least the big ones, are following the good governance practices of a large corporate board. By serving, you will get to see how meetings and committees, such as compensation or audit, are run, and how CEO reviews and committee assessments are conducted. Nonprofit board service affords you the opportunity to showcase your skills and your critical-thinking abilities in front of other board members who might refer you to a for-profit board.

If interested in board service, start working on it in your 50s. Some boards are starting to have term limits; most have age limits, which are usually around 72. A board wants some-one who can serve for at least six to 10 years. Write articles in your area of expertise and get them published for industry magazines or board magazines. Rita was introduced to one of her current boards because of an article that was written about her, and a recruiting firm picked it up in one of their searches. Get out and meet other board members.

Also, have realistic expectations and know what type of board you are searching for. Private company or a private equity–run boards are much more operational by nature. They want someone with a specific expertise who will be very hands-on. A corporate board wants proven executives who will be strategic in their questions and interactions. Yes, you may have been the best in your field, but have realistic expectations. Getting on your first board is hard, and chances are the first won't be a Fortune 100 company. Serving on the right starter board or mid-size cap company can be a great place to start.

Your Business Team of Experts

The challenge of starting a new business or other business activity may require your own Business Team of Experts—including a personal coach, sounding board, lawyer, banker, accountant, and technology expert.

Whether trying out revolutionary or evolutionary things in this new stage of your life, why not consider hiring a personal coach? Make sure you interview several to ensure that you are selecting someone who can work with your style, yet push and challenge you at the same time. If you can't afford hiring a certified coach, see if there is someone whom you respect among your friends who might serve in this role as you shape your business ideas and carry them out. Don't worry; there will be plenty that you can give back in return.

The sounding board is similar. Having several colleagues, family, friends, or acquaintances with whom you can routinely brainstorm or discuss ideas is priceless.

We have made many suggestions in this chapter about people with whom to consult either informally or by hiring them, or even by interning for them. Having a team of your own for your business needs will help enormously in successfully conceiving and realizing your next working phase.

Tying it All Together

Not having to work 60 to 80 hours a week frees you up to think about what's important in life and to live a very rich life. We share Vance's story here as an example of someone who is leading a portfolio career after retirement, one that combines the creative, volunteerism, and work for pay. Vance didn't want to retire when she did. Her husband was ill and needed her to be closer to home and to care for him. While doing so Vance has carved out a post-retirement life that allows her to contribute to and help shape society so that our world is better off.

Having free time opens up volunteering opportunities. When Hurricane Sandy happened, Vance figured out where to call to ask where the most help was needed. That's how she came to work for the Election Board just before the national elections. Dislocated people needed places to vote and needed to be steered in the right direction. Vance also serves on the board of a meditation institute. Through meditation and the work the institute is doing, Vance believes a better world is created.

Vance is making money too as a consultant, and it's all by word of mouth. She uses her marketing and project management skills to help all sorts of companies from large ones like IBM and JPMorgan Chase Bank to small entrepreneurial shops, including the school of entrepreneurship at Columbia University.

You will most likely find that you will do several things during different periods in the years ahead. Bob, now in his 80s, has a reinvention story of what he calls serendipity and so many opportunities.

Bob retired as a three-star American Army general and was overseas on a trip when he expressed to a friend, while dining in Paris, his interest in studying art history in Italy.

The person at the next table overhead him and suggested he go right there in Paris to American University and teach a course and not have to pay tuition. And that's what he did. Later, someone mentioned to him a job where he could direct a grad school in Bologna, Italy, and he did that for five years. Then he was nominated unexpectedly to be president of the Monterey Institute of International Studies and did so for 11 years. Bob is still working. He moved to Washington, DC, where he consults on international security and sits on several nonprofit boards.

What is your path? We hope this chapter has given you new ideas and useful resources to explore in answering this question, now and in the years ahead. The possibilities are endless once you open your mind to considering all the options available, including inventing something uniquely suited for you.

 ## Exercise 4-1: Assessing Your Skills

Regardless of the job titles you had throughout your working career, you had a certain set of skills that make you successful in your work. Reflect on which skills made you successful. Write down in your journal all of those skills. Examples might be: good problem-solving skills, ability to find consensus, sense of humor, and so forth.

- ☐ Ask your friends, partner, former employers, and employees to give you feedback on your skills.
- ☐ Reflect upon how that list of skills might apply to what you decide to do at this stage in life.
- ☐ Ask yourself and others what skills are needed in this new economic environment, which of your skills respond to those needs, and how you can best position yourself for them.

CHAPTER 5

What Will I Do With My Time?

A self that goes on changing is a self that goes on living.

—Virginia Woolf

What am I going to do with all that time?

Many people soon to retire ask themselves that question. And so might you. This chapter talks about the beginning of retirement and the concepts of rebooting and reinvention. Rebooting is a period in which to take a break before plunging into new activities. It's rejuvenation. You'll answer the question *Which paths should I take?* The chapter is divided into two main sections: "Starting Your Retirement" and "Reinvention: The Path Ahead." The reinvention part of this chapter is where you gain all kinds of ideas for pursuing creative endeavors and volunteerism.

Chapter 4: Reinventing Into New Work focused on how you can continue to earn money doing what you enjoy and to supplement your retirement funds. But maybe you're saying to yourself, "Wait a minute! I've earned this free time in my life. I am perfectly happy not having another business career or projects. Spending time with family, with grandchildren, and exercise such as golf, tennis, or yoga and pursuing other pursuits may be exactly I want." There is no one formula. This chapter contains lots of ideas to ponder.

Starting Your Retirement

If there were one major recommendation we have for you upon your retirement, it would be to take time for yourself at the outset. That's right. Take some downtime to reboot, renew, and refresh before you become busy again doing another job, volunteering, or taking on family activities. It is important to have *you* time. Many of us are uncomfortable having free time and no appointments in our lives, but if you spend a little time in that space in the unknown—without lots of commitments to others—you will have time to reacquaint yourself with one of your best retirement buddies: *you!* Take the first couple of months, or even six, to reflect and to do things that you enjoy and didn't have time to do while working.

Tony went down to Florida for a few weeks as soon as he retired from his job at the U.S. Postal Service in Washington, DC, after 37 years there. He relaxed, played golf, and began to catch up with himself. He and his wife felt so in sync and happy. It was a great start. He knew that upon his return to Washington, he'd be doing doctors' appointments, reviewing investments and insurance, organizing things around the house, and generally catching up before he committed to any next steps, including new work. This Florida time was very special and rejuvenating.

Clearing Space

You've been working all your adult years—crazy hours with lots of deadlines and pressures. You are entering a period of preparation for your new life and need to set the groundwork for new experiences. So, start by clearing your calendar and giving yourself time off to focus on getting some things done, as Tony did when he returned to his home in Washington.

After leaving the hectic pace of work and before launching into something new, we and other people in transition first found the need to clear out the clutter in our lives. Creating space both physically and mentally is a key step before moving on to explore other paths. Some people decide that they want to take care of doctor and dental appointments, others to clean out a cluttered room or to take time to go to a spa or meditation center.

The First Thirty Days

We use the term "The First Thirty Days" in our book *Reboot Your Life,* although it doesn't literally have to mean the first 30 days. The period could be a week, a couple of weeks, or more. Or it could be two to three months. It refers to the period when both your body and your mind are transitioning from working full-time to rebooting for your next life chapter. The first 30 days are crucial; they set the stage for your next phase in life.

For many, retirement represents a new beginning, and it's wonderful, but others experience anxiety about the change. It's a shock to the system. It can be a time when you feel raw or unmoored, like a boat adrift in a vast choppy sea. You are accustomed to going to meetings from 8 a.m. to 6 p.m., peppered with other evening obligations, and then what you do at home.

So don't be surprised if you even feel a bit unwell in the early days. You might feel nauseated, have headaches, or find you can't eat. Some report sleeping until noon—and feeling "lazy" for it. Many get colds or flu. In fact, there is science that shows our immune systems are impacted by the change, and we are more vulnerable to illnesses. How many of us have taken a vacation to relax and instead find within the first week that we come down with a cold or the flu? It's the same phenomenon. When we relax, our naturally adrenalin-charged immune systems that serve us well for the pressures of work let go, thus making our bodies relax and more susceptible to illness until they recalibrate.

Many retirees report they do not know what to do with themselves in the beginning. It's not uncommon to experience work or contact withdrawal.

> *Frank struggled with not having a day full of appointments and suffered from a symptom called "e-mail withdrawal." He was no longer on call and in demand.*

Fear is common, too.

> *Gary and Barbara reported feeling guilty not going to work and, in fact, felt terrified that first week. Each had been so used to being scheduled.*

Many have trouble not being in a routine at first and need time to decompress. The loss of structure can feel overwhelming. Retirement can be a shock and a loss of rhythm, rhyme, and reason. Others adjust quickly and happily.

Victor found he needed two or three months to decompress. "Not having a preconceived time schedule is very smart to begin with. Letting go of all the tension from work is a great thing."

Bev, a physician, said, "I loved the joy of not having to be in any one place at a certain time."

And Mary added, "I experienced joy and relief at not having to wake up in the morning and put my presentation face on. I suddenly had a lot less conflict in my life."

Retirement can be a real ego challenge for you. Now that you don't have that big title or job to mention, the questions *Who are you?* and *What do you do?* can be disconcerting when you first retire. Read on—you will find several answers to these concerns.

The first 30 days offer an important time and space to ask: *What do you want for yourself? Are you living well? How many friends and loved ones do you have around? What helps or hinders you on that journey toward living well and living the lifestyle you want?*

Feeding Your Body and Spirit

Feed Your Body

We found people often in the first 30 days started to focus on their bodies and health. If you've been neglecting yourself physically, this is a good time to establish new habits and set goals for your health. That might mean jogging or swing dancing or yoga or just walking out in the fresh air each day. Play golf! Especially after the age of 50, it is critical to do some cardio exercise. Trust us: It helps that tummy roll, too! But cardio doesn't have to be two hours in the gym on machines. Find ways that are fun and work for you.

Maybe this is a time to test yourself physically by running a road race or trying rock climbing (after you touch base with your doctor, of course). If you are going to do this and have not been exercising regularly, do yourself a favor and get one or two lessons with a fitness trainer or take a class at your local YMCA or neighborhood gym offering a free trial period. Learn how to use any equipment properly to avoid injuries.

For more information on living a healthy life, including much more information on exercise, make sure you read **Chapter 8: Most Important of All: Your Health.**

Feed Your Spirit

In addition to your body, explore ways to take care of your mind and spirit. Be in the moment and "smell the flowers," as the saying goes. Take time to explore new, old, or forgotten activities from trying out new foods to taking a dance class to picking up a new sport. Enjoy the little pleasures in life, like reading the newspaper cover to cover, cooking dinner for friends, going to a play, or taking a walk.

Make an "artist date" with yourself. That's where you pursue an activity, any activity, that you do alone and that stimulates your mind and creativity. It could be a visit to a museum, listening to music, sketching something in your neighborhood, discovering a new neighborhood, or taking a walk in the woods. Or just spending an hour in an art supply store. They are fun times—and they are just for you.

Buddhists have been preaching mindfulness, or being in the moment, for thousands of years. It means being fully aware of what is going on inside and outside yourself at any given moment. Mindfulness includes training yourself to put the brakes on and enjoy what's going on right now, to be non-judgmental, and to stop the past and future thoughts and anxieties racing through your head from stealing your present.

Practicing mindfulness can take many forms. It can be a seated or walking meditation or actively enjoying a beautiful or peaceful situation.

Sarah told us:

> *When I wake up in the morning, I give myself a few minutes. The first thing I do is notice that I am breathing. My awareness simply finds my breath. I allow myself to notice the quality of air on my skin, the warmth of the blankets, anything at all. I encourage myself to be vivid, even if it means noticing that my eyes are glued shut with sleepiness and one hip is uncomfortable. I have learned that I do not need to have*

judgmental feelings about myself or the day or my condition. This has been liberating, regardless of whether I'm well or fighting a cold, sleeping late, or getting up very early.

We encourage you to consider creating a daily meditation practice. Meditation is a practice of concentrated focus upon a sound, object, visualization, breathing, movement, or attention itself in order to increase awareness of the present moment, reduce stress, promote relaxation, and enhance personal and spiritual growth. Whereas mindfulness is simple and concrete—paying attention, on purpose, and in the moment—meditation can be a million different things. It can even include prayer and chanting or just sitting still. The benefits are enormous.

Bob says, "Meditation reduces my anxiety by slowing things down. It gives me energy and makes me feel better physically. I am lighter and more able to concentrate. Optimism is more present for me."

Use this wonderful stage of your life to practice being in the moment. Even as you are out and about, doing errands or going to a meeting, look around you, enjoy the moment fully and try to "find beauty" in every day and in the smallest things.

Reconnection

Up until now, we've talked about a few ways you can reconnect with yourself in those first 30 days.

This is also a time to reconnect with friends and family, especially people you have not had a chance to see during your busy working days. This is a good time for a family reunion or to travel around the country to visit family and friends.

There are so many fun ways to reconnect with that part of you that had to be put aside because of the demands of your career. Make it a mission to find all of the fun and free things to do in your city or town with your grandchildren. One person with whom we spoke started a photography project with his grandson. They drove around their neighborhood and nearby finding funny mailboxes to photograph and then created a book that the grandchild took to school. Here's another idea.

Grace plans a family reunion with her stepchildren every other year in a place that is wonderful for the adults as well as the children. She rents a huge house so they all stay together. She organizes shared cooking and cleaning up and plans "girls" events, as well as sports events, for the family. They go for two weeks and have been to Cape Cod, a camp in Minnesota, and France, and on a cruise.

We heard of many others doing these "extended family vacations" and think they are part of a new trend.

When was the last time you called a friend for lunch or dinner? If you have been working the hours we suspect you have, you probably see friends over a quiet lunch all too infrequently. Whether they are still working or not, they will be delighted to get the call from you. Start by making a list of all of your friends and family with whom you have missed spending more time. Where would you want to start?

Planning trips with friends around an activity to keep you all fit is another, multi-benefit adventure. Tennis camps, golf outings, bike clubs—all offer fun ways to travel with exercise and camaraderie built in.

A novel way to stay in touch with friends was created by a group of our Reboot Your Life Retreat participants. They formed a book club, which meets via a free conference call for an hour and a half every two months. The call also includes catching up with each other's news. The group has become so close that they now plan annual reunions.

Seeing someone face-to-face is always the best, but modern technology is providing some good free or inexpensive alternatives for connecting with friends and family. Skype, which allows you to see each other on video, is free for members and costs pennies when calling into a regular number. Tango, another tool, is what our grandchildren might be using and is easy to connect to. Facetime from Apple is a fast-growing application and services like www.freeconferencecalling.com let you conference a few friends to talk together and share your lives.

Many of us focused so much on work that we had little time to cultivate our old friendships, and many fell by the wayside.

This may be a time to build new friendships and build a new community of support for you through interests you may have and share with others. You can do that by joining local associations related to your interests, playing tennis and being matched with someone you don't yet know, taking exercise classes, or participating in community mixers where networking and getting to know each other is part of the experience. Don't be afraid; there are so many people in the same situation looking for new friendships and community.

Being with family and friends can be the most reaffirming part of this new phase in your life. It solidifies the base of who you are and what you care about.

Travel and Exploration

After your initial time off focused on your mind and body, it's time to continue exploring and having fun. When was the last time you visited a local museum? What other interesting places are nearby that you have never even visited? Where have you wanted to go elsewhere in your country or far away? Many of us use the beginning of our freedom for travel, both near and afar.

For so many of us, there was just never enough time for vacation and particularly for travel. Were you that way? Or perhaps you were like Roger?

> *Roger's job entailed traveling all over the world—to amazing places—but while there, he barely saw anything. He worked the whole time, including evenings, and then, guilt ridden about being away, rushed back home to be with his family. He never extended his time even a day to see the magical sites, people, and cultures of a different land.*

Now is the time to travel to all those places you have dreamed of visiting. And it doesn't have to cost a lot of money.

Reinvention: The Path Ahead

You've now, hopefully, had time off to relax, get back in shape, reconnect with friends and family, and maybe travel and experience that magical place you have been dreaming about for years. Now, what do you want to do with your life? As we said before, it's okay to say that relaxing is exactly what you want to continue doing. Or some of you may have already started in a new job or other major activity. Following, we address the kinds of ongoing activities that recharge your batteries outside of work. These are opportunities for reinvention.

When Americans meet new people in the United States, less so in other countries, the first question someone asks is *What do you do?* Most of us have come to identify our "self" with a job title, a company, or an industry. But that's not *you*—not the inner you. It's an important part of your life and no one can ever take that away from you, but now is the time to become acquainted with "the other you."

The same leadership skills you exhibited in work might suit you well doing a volunteer activity. Perhaps there's a creative side to you that has been hidden away since childhood. Or one that believes it is time for you to give back and get involved in your local community. Don't feel you have to figure out the next 30 years. What would you like to do for the next few months, year, or couple of years?

> *Upon retirement, Mark moved to his dream city, Rio de Janeiro. He took a course and became a certified tour guide so that he could fully get to know his new city and the richness of its history. Then, he chose to spend his time on non-paying activities: working on the Nature Conservancy board and for Pro Mujer, a Latin American–based women's health and microfinance organization. He shared, "I am invigorated with the fact that I don't know what I will be doing in four or five years. But, I know it will be an exciting ride, and I love the possibilities and how I get to keep reinventing myself."*

> *Gene was a senior executive for a major insurance company and spent much of his time on corporate finance and budgeting. He has translated those skills to help low income people and seniors do their tax returns. He says it is so fulfilling and gratifying to take what he knows, and was paid for in his corporate life, and give back to others.*

What will make you feel relevant, fulfilled, and jazz you up for this next phase of your life?

There is no fixed formula for what is right for you. You will know it when you see it or feel it. The important thing is to use the first six months to a year of your retirement to experiment and try lots of different things.

These could be things that you did as a kid, things you've always wanted to do but never had the time to do, things that you never dreamed you could do, and even things that scare you.

Mike told us:

"I thought I was allergic to writing. Sure, in my position, I had to write a lot for work. And I was as good as anyone else in business writing or writing a motivational speech. But creative writing or writing a book—hah—never me. I am now writing a book about four generations running a successful business. Gosh, it was painful at first. But I love to tell stories, especially when the story can liberate someone else. Bit by bit, I now identify myself as a writer. So, my advice is don't shy away from ideas you perceive as weird or scary."

Whether you want to pursue creative endeavors, volunteer, or run for a political or public policy position, take time to visualize your next endeavor in your mind, as if you were already doing it really successfully. Remember our visualization exercise in the planning chapter? Do it again now.

It's okay, too, to combine a few things you want to do. Rita calls that leading a "portfolio life." Rita retired nine years ago and today, when asked what she does, replies:

"I lead a portfolio life. One third of my time is spent volunteering, one third is spent serving on corporate boards and coaching people how to get on corporate boards (which funds the volunteer work), and one third is on having fun—travel, photography, and writing this book."

This reinvention period can also be a time of learning. Perhaps you want to go back to school, learn a new language, get your pilot's license, or learn to scuba dive. Maybe it's a time to explore a new hobby like restoring an old car, gardening, making quilts, or writing a novel.

If you have worked in one or two positions all of your adult life, it's hard to know all the myriad things one can do to keep busy and fulfilled. We welcome you to share your ideas with us on our Website (*www.revolutionary-retirement.com*). In the meantime, read ahead for ideas on volunteerism and creative endeavors.

Volunteering

Volunteering is good for your health. That's right, it's good for your health because you gain back more than you give. There is no better way to "get out of yourself"—to lose your worries or concerns. You become totally immersed in someone else's life, not yours. Plus, you've been blessed in life. You have skills that someone else is in need of, and there are so many deserving people and causes that need you.

We each spend a good portion of our time doing volunteer work. Nancy is an expert in conflict resolution and has spent time on several nonprofit boards. Jaye spends significant time working for a locally based child welfare agency where she has been on the board for many years.

Rita retired early so that she could make volunteering a large part of her life—that third of her portfolio career. She says:

"I worked 60-hour weeks and lived on a plane. I was yearning to do some sort of volunteer work, and I woke up one day with the realization that the only way I was going to be able to do that was to make it a major part of my life, which necessitated retiring early. The organization in which I immersed myself right after retiring was Pro Mujer. I became chair of the board, worked at least 17 hours a week in the early days of our formation, traveled all over Latin America to meet about microfinance and health with the most wonderful women and their families, all of whom lived on under $2 a day, and loved every minute of it—well almost all. Volunteering is not without its challenges and frustrations."

Cathy's story is a little different.

Once people heard that Cathy was retiring from a financial consortium, and moving back to Santa Fe from Washington, DC, nonprofit organizations came out of the woodwork asking her to join their boards or various causes. Cathy says she is a good example of someone who accepted too many offers too quickly and soon found that she had too much on her plate. On overload, she had to recalibrate and stay active in only those organizations that met her passions and where she felt she could make a difference.

Chapter 6: Retirement Robbers and Other Challenges further addresses overload, which is one of the dangers when you retire. It's good to go slowly, research, visit the organizations, and pick just a couple of things to commit to before jumping ahead and taking on too much.

Volunteering comes in all shapes and sizes. Reading to someone in a hospital or assisted-living home for even one hour means so much to the recipient. You can tutor at a local school or in an underprivileged neighborhood. Look into Communities in Schools for opportunities in your locale.

> *Cora is an energetic 85-year-old who reads to refugee students at an elementary school in Boise, Idaho. The reading improves the students' skills and self-confidence, and Cora becomes a role model/ grandma figure/teacher all rolled up in one. The one-on-one lunches can be especially influential. And, how she loves doing it!*

Food banks need volunteers every day. You can tap into your interests and network to explore different places where you'd like to volunteer regularly, perhaps once a week or month. Or, you can find opportunities that take only a day. Nathaniel spent a day building a house with Habitat for Humanity after Hurricane Katrina.

There are services that match volunteers. Every nonprofit in which you might be interested has a Website with a section on how to volunteer there. Check them out and see what strikes you and peaks an interest or passion.

Becoming a Nonprofit Board Member

Becoming a member of a nonprofit organization board can be a meaningful way to explore how your own experience and expertise can be applied to the nonprofit sector. It can also be a rewarding way to get to know other people in your community, though it can be very time-consuming and require a long-term commitment.

How do you go about identifying board opportunities? Individuals often choose a particular cause because they know someone already associated with it. If you don't know where you might want to serve, organizations that do board matching include *www.boardnetusa.org* and BoardSource (*www.boardsource.org*).

It's important to choose causes about which you are most passionate. Serving on a not-for-profit board is a big commitment of time, and you are then an ambassador to the cause. You will most likely be asked to contribute financially as well.

> *Pam was going through two transitions: retiring and moving to a new community. She wanted to use her newfound time and business skills to serve on a nonprofit board. But determining which one wanted her and which one she wanted was a quandary. Quickly she decided that it was important to choose a local organization so that she could meet other interesting people in her area. She did research on the web, creating a list of local organizations. Then she narrowed the list down by selecting those causes for which she had a passion. She researched who was on each board and found ways to be introduced to one of the board members. The process of due diligence took more than six months, but she was thrilled when she was asked to be on the board of one of our country's nicest botanical gardens.*

Determining Which Opportunities Are Best for You

You should treat finding the right organization with which to do volunteer work, especially board service, the same way you did when looking for full-time employment. Make sure you do proper due diligence. Understand their financials and the potential liabilities of the board. Start by going to some of the organization's events. See if you can volunteer for a day or shadow one of their workers. Inquire if you can go on a donor trip. Doing so is a great way to see the inner workings of an organization, meet clients, and meet the local staff.

Once you've checked out the financials and the organization's reputation and done your due diligence, ask these questions:

1. Are my goals and those of the institution aligned?

2. Do I have the right set of skills, experience, and expertise that will help advance the mission of the organization, and will my contributions be valued?

3. Am I prepared to commit the time required to meet my duties as a trustee?

4. Am I willing to have my name and my reputation associated with this organization?

5. Am I in a position to give and raise money for this cause?

Public Service and Activism

There are many ways to get civically involved and lend a hand. Perhaps you want to volunteer for hurricane relief with our national fisheries or be a teacher at sea. Or you may want to serve on a committee in your local community, such as the finance board or the local school board.

A good place to start your exploration is on the Internet at sites like *www.serve.gov*, *www.nationalservice.gov*, and, for opportunities outside the United States, *www.crossculturalsolutions.org*. Consider joining the Service Corps of Retired Executives (SCORE), AmeriCorps, or Senior Corps.

Serving your government provides valuable community services so that more money can be spent on local improvement. At the same time, it's good for you. Civic service provides physical and mental rewards. Consider serving on the economic development board, volunteering for your local fire department, or getting involved some way in local politics or a local organization. Experts report that focusing on someone other than yourself interrupts tension-producing patterns and makes you happier while building self-esteem.

You have arrived at an age of wisdom and now is the time—some think your duty—to share your authentic voice. Whether you worked for corporations or the public sector as an employee, you always had to be a bit careful of what you said and how you said it. Now that you are free to share your voice, it is a good time to consider actively advancing causes you believe in. Chris, for example, has chosen in her retirement to be an activist for women's issues. Mark advocates for gay rights and the environment. Think of the causes that are important to you and the world. Climate change? Racism? Economic development? Microfinancing? Education? You, too, might choose to be an activist for a cause about which you care passionately.

Volunteer Travel

Many people enjoy combining volunteer work with travel. You can immerse yourself in wonderful places for a week, a month, a couple of months, or longer. Many of us wanted to work with the Peace Corps in our 20s. Did you know that the Peace Corps now offers a two-month program in addition to its traditional two-year commitment? Like to be in the outdoors? Work in exchange for food and board or an RV hookup at one of the United States National Parks. Prefer to see countries you've never visited? Have a particular cause in mind? Not to worry, opportunities exist. The Appendix lists Websites to help you with your exploration.

The sky is the limit, as Helen, a retired Wall Street executive, can attest:

> *"Never would I have predicted that I would travel to Bhutan then return to become a teacher of young Buddhist monks. First friends invited me to travel with them to Bhutan. The next year, I helped our tour guide and his wife become exhibitors at a show in the U.S., and one thing led to another. I was presented with the opportunity to teach in Bhutan for two years. Why not? I had recently split from my partner and had no obligations. The experiences I had during that year were immeasurable treasures—ones that I will always hold near to my heart. I have been enriched in many, many ways."*

There are one-week, one-month, and two-month options to volunteer abroad, too. You might want to combine an opportunity to give back with a family vacation as Maggie and Stephan did with their children and grandchildren. Maggie tells the story:

> *"I was ready to retire and wanted to do a volunteer gig overseas with my husband, Stephan, who would be retiring around the same time. We had always loved volunteering and travel, so were looking for opportunities to combine the two overseas. Bingo! We could volunteer in South Korea for two months and invite our two Korean-born grandchildren to visit us there to learn more about their original culture. In the end, the kids' parents and other relatives joined us for part of the time, too. What a great experience for all!"*

Special Resources

We mentioned Encore.org in the last chapter as a career resource. It also is a good resource for you for ideas of how to shift from your career work to solving challenging social problems of our time, including poverty, the environment, education, and healthcare.

Among the huge number of AARP resources to help navigate retirement is *www.aarp.org/giving-back*, which is designed to help you find a way to make a difference in your community.

No matter what our circumstances may be, there is always someone worse off than we are. We have been blessed with skills and talents from which someone out there would benefit. And sharing those skills is good for your health and well-being. It gets you thinking of something beyond yourself and, in so doing, makes you feel great.

Walk on the Creative Side

We are all born to be creative. Yes, that means you. You are creative. You just may not have exercised that muscle in many years. Most of us feel that we need to squash that side of our brain or put it aside, as if it is not needed in jobs. Children are universally creative, and that's how they approach the world, but as adults we often lose that freedom and flexibility of mind.

You might want to explore your creative side by taking a workshop. One that we've tried and like is The Creativity Workshop (*www.creativity-workshop.com*). In a fun, collaborative setting through playing and assignments in all sorts of mediums—storytelling, writing, photography, drawing, and collage—you learn practical techniques to stimulate creativity and imagination and how to overcome creative blocks. Many workshops are offered at fun places around the world at reasonable rates, so you can exercise your creative muscle and scratch that itch to travel all at once!

And check your local community college or university, as they are creating noncredit courses for new learners.

Photography

Photography presents a way to view our world differently. And in so doing, we get to combine technology with art, thus forming a wonderful creative outlet.

When Jim retired, he dove into the sports that he never had the time to do while working. He played tennis and golf several times a week and, as an avid biker, rode many hours a week. He was immediately recruited to serve on some non-profit boards in his hometown of Rochester, NY, which he did gladly. But the activity he likes the most is photography, a hobby he had lost touch with as an adult.

He started his travel photography with landscapes and monuments. But when he got home, it was always the pictures of people that meant the most, because they really captured the spirit of the place. He has been to nearly 40 countries. The more remote and the less explored, the better for him.

Nancy's love of horses led her to take a photography course on an Idaho ranch, then one on a Wyoming ranch, then in France. She has some wonderful horse portraits and scenic shots of horses running. Rita took many sunrise and sunset shots over the harbor and oceans of Martha's Vineyard at an Alison Shaw workshop that she also highly recommends. Other workshops and photo-related sites are listed in the Appendix.

Writing

There are approximately 200 writing conferences a year in the United States alone. That gives you a lot of options, so take your time, do some research, and see what a particular conference has to offer and where it is. If possible, use Google to find testimonials from writers who have been there, and pay attention to what they liked and disliked about an event. Cathy recommends the Cape Cod Writers Center Conference that happens every August, as well as workshops in Santa Fe, New Mexico, a hot spot for creativity.

You can also select courses close to home. Your local community college or university will most likely offer options. Or you may want to use this as a chance to combine travel and exploration to a new part of the country. Some programs specialize in writing about kids, mystery, romance, or non-fiction. Some are also online and can be done inexpensively from the comfort of your own home.

Besides your local schools and colleges, *writingclasses.com*, *writersinstitute.gc.cuny.edu*, *writersstudio.com*, and the University of Iowa's writing program are just a few of the places to explore.

Cooking

Many of us found ourselves in jobs for years where we could only—or were expected only—to use our left brain, the analytical and logical side of our brain. Deep inside, we may have been yearning to unlock the creative within. Cooking is a great way to do so. There is so much creativity and fun in experimenting and trying new cuisines and ingredients.

> *Ray was a successful trial lawyer. The work was stimulating and rewarding, both intellectually and financially, but it was also exhausting. Toward the end of his career, he was drained emotionally. Once retired, he wanted to spend his waking hours doing something totally different. He loves to read and travel and, when at home, he loves to cook. Friends had frequently raved about his cooking, especially his desserts. So this hotshot lawyer decided to go back to school as a student—to culinary school. Today, besides making his wife and friends fabulous meals, he sells gluten-free brownies and chocolate macaroons to specialty shops in Los Angeles.*

Many of you may want to take courses, not because you want another paying job but simply for enjoyment. There are all sorts of courses ranging from a few hours to weekend intensives to longer certified culinary programs. Perhaps you want to combine your cooking passion with a vacation in the relaxed environment of a country house in France, or on a remote Greek island, or at a Venetian palace with plenty of time for market tours, wine tastings, and leisurely meals. Or look for a specialty cooking school near you. For a list of some culinary programs, see the Appendix.

Other Creative Endeavors

There are so many other ways to stretch your imagination, your innovation, and your creativity. Furniture making, for example, can be explored by taking a carpentry course at a tech college near you or by going online to learn at your own pace in your own home.

The same holds true for other activities. If you have ever wanted to nurture your creative abilities through a class but don't know where to begin, start right now by looking at your own city. Local schools and universities and other nonprofit organizations are filled with courses where people of all learning levels and artistic abilities can explore their own hidden talents. Check the Internet, too. There are myriad courses, such as ceramics, silk-screening, drawing, painting, antique car repair, letterpress design, and more. If you don't see a creative outlet that resonates with you, keep dreaming and searching. There's a potential new life path right around the corner waiting for you.

There are so many options for us in retirement that we often use the phrases *saving the best for last* and *the next and best chapter* to express the joy we find in ourselves and others at finally having time to follow our passions. We hope you will too!

 Exercise 5-1: Small Risks

Select two or three categories of things that you have never done, haven't done recently, or would like to try, but have been afraid to. Get a little out of your comfort zone.

☐ For each category, list five things you will do in the next three to six months. Examples might include: five places to visit in your local city, five foods you would like to cook, or five new forms of exercise or exercise classes you want to try out.

CHAPTER 6

Retirement Robbers and
Other Challenges

*The years between fifty and seventy are the hardest. You
are always asked to do things, and you are not yet decrepit
enough to turn them down.*

—T.S. Eliot

You have just retired and the requests are coming in. Because of the use of the word *retirement,* everyone thinks you have plenty of time on your hands. Can you babysit the grandchild this summer three times a week? Can you walk the dog for us during the day? Will you be on our non-profit board or chair the fundraising event? Will you teach Sunday School at our church? Your new lifestyle is about to be challenged by others' agendas. And, unfortunately, most often by *you* responding to those agendas or creating ones of your own that take you off course!

We call these challenges Retirement Robbers, just as we called them Sabbatical Robbers in our book *Reboot Your Life.* The Robbers are intrusions and demands from you or others into the plans that you have created for this next chapter in life. These intrusions and demands can cause you to use your time less effectively and not live the life you envision. Let's look at some of the Robbers that can come up, both external and internal.

External Robbers

You will recognize these. They are people and circumstances that affect you. Some can be anticipated; others come at you without much warning. As you will read later in this chapter, you may not perceive all of these as Robbers at first.

Here are some examples, which we introduce here and expand on as this chapter progresses:

* **Requests for your time and commitment,** likely a mixture of welcome requests and those that are not so welcome.

* **The economy and other economic concerns,** diminishing your nest egg or causing worry about it, resulting in your continuing to work to earn income whether you want to or not.

* **Bad luck related to your health or that of your loved ones,** such as developing a chronic disease or disability.

* **"Sandwich generation" responsibilities**—financial and time demands from your parents and children. Baby Boomers can be caught in the middle, draining their own retirement dreams and finances, at least temporarily.

* **Your spouse at home,** who would like more of your time.

* **Crazymakers:** people who suck up your energy and time with excessive focus on themselves.

Internal Robbers

Internal Robbers are those you create yourself. Often we create barriers to our own dreams because we believe we don't really deserve them. Here are some examples, which are covered in more depth as we go along:

* **Procrastination on doing anything due to various fears,** including timidity about planning or realizing your dreams, working too long at your lifetime job (beyond what you really want), fear of economic downturn, or fear of being viewed as irrelevant.

* **Poor health and physical ability because you don't exercise and take care of yourself** creates more likelihood of loss of options or curtailing of activity. Unavoidable health problems are not in this category.

* **You can't say no,** creating an imbalance in your life—that is, doing a lot of what you don't want to do.

* **You want to do it all,** so you do not make decisions and plan. You dabble in lots of activities but are finding it hard to move forward in a well thought-out manner.

* **Guilt.** *Should I really be doing all these things I love? Shouldn't I still be working or volunteering more?* This can be an outsized detractor that can hinder progress on designing and living the life you want.

We also will talk about losing one's spouse and single life, which can be a lonely time with no constant companion for the dreamed-of travel and exciting new life after full-time work.

Not All Potential Robbers Are Robbers

Is everything that comes up unexpectedly a Retirement Robber? No! These requests may be exactly what you would love to do, such as volunteering or spending time with a grandchild. Volunteering can lead to other exciting opportunities. And, we know that babysitting can be a joy—unless it becomes an obligation and expectation by the child's parents that takes away from your own time and other plans. You have to make that assessment, and it may change over time.

Let's take an example. You are officially retired from your lifetime career and have a busy life planned with travel, classes, lunches with friends, and potentially some part-time consulting. Your son asks you to babysit your 5-year-old granddaughter, Tina, full-time all summer until school starts again in the fall. Ouch! That means going over to their house every day, no breaks during the day to run errands or have lunch out, no classes unless in the evening, and nothing getting done at home. What about all those closets and drawers you were going to tackle? Or the consulting opportunities you wanted to explore? Or investigating other places to live?

What do you do? Of course you want to spend time with Tina, but maybe there is a middle ground. What about having her at your apartment? What about three days a week instead of five? What about working with her parents to find a pre-school or part-time playgroup? What about deferring your taking classes until the fall? With these possibilities, you get to turn a potential Retirement Robber into a retirement joy as you further build your relationship with this little girl and help her parents out as well.

The Role of Timing

Robbers are seen differently at different times. Remember that you are entering a new life chapter, and it is likely that you still have more chapters to go. The requests that flood in as soon as you post the "retirement" sign will lessen as you figure out your priorities and take a stand on them. And when a request comes up again, it may be perfect timing.

Other types of requests for your time, such as volunteer activities, may be an intrusion early on and welcome later, or vice versa.

Barbara, a lifelong educator, retired as a high school principal and plunged into volunteer activities. She helped older people with their needs, worked with several community organizations, mentored, and sponsored an annual scholarship for single mothers studying business. She welcomed all these requests and activities into her life and did not consider them infringements on her free time. Later, she cut back to providing the scholarship and staying in touch with the recipients. She decided she'd rather preserve her energy to read, be with friends, and take care of her house and the neighbor's dog.

Dealing With External Robbers

If you are aware of potential Robbers and other situations that could keep you from the lifestyle you seek or from meeting your goals, you can be ready to deal with them.

Requests for Your Time

Every day will bring external requests for your time. Your time is a valuable commodity, and you will want to be able to assess fully how to spend it, including the important flexible time for *you*. Requests will come from your family, your friends, neighbors, colleagues, professional groups, and nonprofit groups. They may come directly to you by phone, e-mail, social media, or in person. Or perhaps you will see a general request for involvement, such as a campaign for a cause. It may be a one-time request or a plea for a regular commitment.

Sometimes the request is a personal request from a friend or colleague or family member for help. You can decide how much time (and money) to spend. In some cases, you will be asked for assistance and/or advice. Mentoring is a wonderful way to give back, and you may choose to do that.

> *When Jon retired from his business career, he wanted to travel, do some consulting, and try his hand at writing short stories. He was met with a flood of requests for advice—pro bono—for a number of worthy organizations, including being on standing committees that met frequently. Though he wanted to give back, he had a dilemma and decided to take on individual requests for personal mentoring but not institutional requests, so he could have more control over his time.*

Assessment, Balance, and Boundaries

If the request is direct and personalized to you, you need to decide how to answer. If it is a general opportunity that has caught your attention—such as a community event, political campaign, or cause—you still need to decide, but the pressure is less. In both cases, the decision process includes assessment, balance, and boundaries.

First, you have to figure out if this request fits in the lifestyle you have chosen and into your plan. Or maybe it is a new direction that you want to take or strikes a chord in you. Take the time to visualize yourself doing the activity, including its frequency and the amount of time it will take to include preparation, travel time, and so forth. Be realistic. Is this how you want to spend that chunk of time? The important thing is to have a clear idea of how you want to spend your time and how that activity fits in. How would it enhance your life and goals? What would you have to give up in order to have time to do this?

How would the activity contribute to or pull down your life balance? Would it be your third or fourth volunteer commitment? Is it likely to be too much of a drain on your free time or time with family and friends? It may be just the opposite and be something that pulls your life into better balance. You have to assess.

If you have been setting goals, you are in good shape, and now is the time to add boundaries. Setting boundaries, such as a ceiling on the number of your volunteer activities or babysitting, allows you to say yes to some requests in alignment with your priorities.

Jacqueline, a retired HR officer, does this regarding mentoring requests:

"I get a couple requests a week for mentoring, often about a job search. It is part of my purpose in life, but I simply can't do it all. Many ask if I'll have lunch, and I always say no to that. Then I say, 'Let's start with a 15-minute phone call, and I will give you an assignment in advance to make it meaningful. It helps me know who to make an effort for. Often they don't want to do the assignment, and I don't hear back from them."

Learning to Say No

Many times, you will want to say yes. But, if you want to say no—or want time to think about a request—you will need at least three elements. First, you need a polite and gracious answer to the question. Here are some responses:

* **You can ask for more time to think,** which is a fair request: "Thank you so much. I'm flattered and interested but would like time to consider it."

* **You can suggest someone else:** "I am so sorry; I just can't take on another commitment, but I know a good person for you and will be happy to set up a time for you to meet her."

* **You can declare time off from such activity:** "You are so thoughtful to think of me for this, but this year I am taking a sabbatical from all volunteer work. Please do keep me in mind for next year!"

Second, you will need a way to put your response in a broader context—the context of your life and priorities. So, it is good to have a prepared description of how you are choosing to spend your time—an "elevator speech." An elevator speech is a brief description of your targeted lifestyle and priorities. People may think you have lots of free time, and your explanation of your lifestyle, activities, and priorities can be quite helpful in illuminating your reaction to requests—both for you and the person to whom you are responding.

Craig's "elevator speech" of what he is doing in retirement goes like this:

> *I take biology students to Hawaii as I did when I was teaching. I serve as an "advisor" to my son's organic vegetable garden business, and I play golf with a group once a week all year long. Patty and I stay busy, too, with our delightful grandkids and special travels. My days are full.*

Third is the will to say no, which often can be difficult because we don't like to disappoint others. It is easy to be convinced or flattered into something. Try saying no when someone says you are the only person talented enough to run a particular neighborhood, state, or national activity! You might think, *Really, me? Well, in that case, maybe I should do it.* If you really don't want to do it, you have your planning, goals, priorities, and boundaries to employ. Figure out what you are going to say, practice in front of a mirror if that helps, and then say it with all sincerity and grace. If you want to leave the door open for later, go ahead and do that. But don't let the flattery take you off track and away from your goals.

The Economy and Your Finances and Working

Economic concerns definitely can be a Retirement Robber. Worries about having enough money can take the wind out of your sails, cause fear, and keep you working.

With the information in **Chapter 3: Making Your Money Last** and **Chapter 4: Reinventing Into New Work** about financial issues and ways of bringing in an income linked to a passion in mind, you can look for a way to continue working with less chance that work will be a Retirement Robber.

Health: When Chronic Illness or Disability Strikes

We are the first to say that illness and disability can strike you or a loved one totally unexpectedly. It can be a big interruption of your dreams, changing the way you will live your life, either short-term or long-term.

Our first suggestion is always to do what you can to prevent illness and disability through the lifestyle you adopt. But, when faced with adversity, can you see a silver lining? Maybe it means spending more time with an ill mother or other loved one. Maybe it gives you an opportunity to take up a new, less physically demanding hobby or exercise. Maybe it allows you to tune up other aspects of your health while you battle the problem. See if you can find the silver lining and adjust your thinking from Retirement Robber to something more positive. Undoubtedly that path can be extremely challenging, but with the assistance of your own internal resources, friends, family, and other supporters, you can move forward. Believe that you can still have dreams and fulfill them.

Don't be reluctant to bring in help for you or others. There are elder-care specialists who can advise you about resources, available aid, and how to get insurance to pay for additional services. You might need to hire a part-time aide or caretaker to give you a break, or a physical therapist, or you can find support groups for special circumstances. You can also take classes that will give you information to help understand what you can do to better help yourself or a loved one cope better.

Sandwich Generation

What about when your dreams of a new lifestyle are curtailed or delayed by demands of your elderly parents or boomerang children or grandchildren? The "sandwich generation" refers to providing a home for and/or or helping finance your parents and children. Yes, that can be a Retirement Robber! Even if it is only half the sandwich—parents or children—you and your resources are stretched, and you may ask, *What about me? When is it finally my time for my life?*

It can be overwhelming to be caring for an elderly parent. If you are the sibling who lives geographically closest, you probably carry the biggest load. It's hard to get away to travel or to do your own thing.

What to Do About Sandwich Generation Issues

You may have to adopt an interim strategy, starting with assessing the extent to which the situation is a Robber and whether there are strategies to mitigate it. Clearly, it can be a joy to spend extra time with your loved ones, but the financial and time burden can become onerous. And, with your parents, at least the time commitment is likely to increase as they age. Some suggestions follow for both the time and resource issues, as well as some coaching for that younger generation:

✸ **Spreading the responsibilities can be a good strategy.** Regarding your parents, perhaps you have siblings with whom you can split expenses and time demands. Some siblings actually make assignments: *Okay, you take Mom to her doctors' appointments, and I will handle her financial transactions. If her money runs out, we will share the expense.* Sometimes friends will want to help with the time responsibilities, such as driving to appointments or keeping company. You do need a break. You have to nourish yourself to be able to nourish others!

✸ **Talk with your children and parents about setting boundaries** for money and time demands. You may be able to spend less time or money than expected if you plan together with the other members of your household.

✸ **If your adult children are having trouble establishing financial independence, you may find yourself designing strategies** to wean them from your financial care as well as to counsel them on their job search. Our philosophy follows the well-known Chinese proverb: "If you give a man a fish, you feed him for a day. If you teach a man to fish, you feed him for a lifetime." This can apply to life skills, such as cooking, job-seeking, and other activities.

✳ While painful, you may have to tell your child to move out. He or she may have to get an hourly job until something more substantial can be found. Your children later will thank you for recognizing their adulthood by steps you take to help them earn money or get a full-time job.

After two years, Eric had to give his son, Nate, two months to get a job—even at McDonald's—and to move out of the house. It's the best thing that ever happened to Nate.

* Help with their resume and use your contacts. Or, if that is a non-starter with your son or daughter, put him or her in touch with one of your friends who can help.

* At your own pace, you can cut back on what you provide.

* How long do you need to pay the car insurance or car payment? Perhaps you and your child could decide together. You just need to have an expectation that change can come positively. It's a joint project. Nurture it along.

Chapter 3: Making Your Money Last, Chapter 7: Renegotiating Life at Home, and **Chapter 8: Most Important of All: Your Health** cover other aspects of issues related to the Sandwich Generation.

Spouse at Home

Quite a few people we interviewed told us that the biggest Robber is the spouse at home. Yes, we love them and love spending time with them, but they can absorb all your time. You can feel trapped. Your spouse may rely on you for a social network or be possessive, issues that can become apparent early in a retirement. Or you may be doing it to your spouse and not getting out enough on your own!

You both need a plan! **Chapter 7: Renegotiating Life at Home** is devoted to relationships at home, including this dilemma.

Crazymakers

You know them. They are the people who create drama around everything, especially themselves. They stir up storms. Everything is on deadline—an emergency that requires your attention and pulls you off track. Your agenda is less important than theirs.

Jessica and Jane, who had been friends while their children were growing up, were co-chairing a local event. Jane had always had a flair for dramatic reaction, but now all that was in high gear. She constantly missed meetings or arrived late and disrupted everything when she flounced in. The excuse could be a flat tire, her daughter's needs, her grandchild's sniffles, the rude clerk, a technology break-down. She always had a long explanation and, usually, a favor to ask. It was hard for Jessica to focus on the work at hand. She was frustrated and wanted Jane to share the load, but that wasn't hap-pening. Jessica's fretting over it all was getting in the way of progress, too. After the event, Jessica cut back on time spent with Jane because she realized it was unsatisfying and sapping too much of her energy.

You may have somehow bonded with someone like Jane. You find yourself falling short or avoiding what you need to be doing because you are focusing on what the crazymaker needs. You are selling yourself short, and now you need an exit.

We suggest assessing the situation and its effect on you, then setting boundaries for the crazymaker. Explain the problems to her and how her attitude is causing problems for you and pulling you off track. The boundary can be that you will help her one more time, or something else that will prompt a change in behavior.

Dealing with Internal Robbers

Procrastination

Why do we procrastinate? We all do. The path to one's full next chapter can be pockmarked with procrastination. That's not all bad, as rushing precipitously into the future can cause unwanted problems. That's why we keep emphasizing the importance of planning. But, there's a point between rushing too fast and putting on the brakes too vigorously and exclaiming excuses too loudly. If procrastination interferes too much with progress and realizing one's dreams, it is a Retirement Robber.

How and Why We Procrastinate

It is good to learn to recognize if you are procrastinating and to examine the reasons why.

* **Timidity** can keep you from moving forward with planning your dreams. You may lack self-confidence or certainty about your chosen path. You may want more confirmation, endorsement, or encouragement from others.

* **Perfectionism** can bedevil so many of us. We block our-selves from forward movement or keep redoing our plans to get them just right. We seek perfect circumstances. *Just a little more research, or I'll wait until I've lost weight, or I'll check with six more friends.*

* **Fear** can go hand in hand with procrastination. It can be fear of failure, fear of the future or something new, fear of the impact on others, even fear of success. It can be fear about your future relevance and fulfillment or fear of inadequate resources. Such fears place a clammy hand on your shoulder, holding you back from engaging in your own future.

* **Working too long** is a form of procrastination. You will sense when it is time to move on, but if you are unable to acknowledge that it is time and just keep putting off a deci-sion, you are procrastinating. And time is slipping away.

* **Maybe you don't really want to do what you planned,** so you procrastinate. If this is true, you most likely will lack motivation to move forward.

* **Lack of adequate planning** can mean lack of firm grounding on which to move forward. No wonder you procrastinate.

Responses to Procrastination

It is good to understand why you procrastinate and what you can do to get around it. Your procrastination may be well-founded, or at least partially well-founded. It may mainly be caution, but you should learn to assess whether it is caution, lack of planning, or simply stalling.

* **Try to figure out why you are procrastinating.** For exam-ple, if you have fears about letting go of what feels familiar and safe, remember at one time what you are doing now was new and different, and you managed quite well.

* **Set boundaries for yourself**—for example: *I will decide by November 6. I will act by the end of the year. I will not do B until I do A.*

❋ **Decide what you need/lack to go forward,** then make a plan to get and do what you need.

❋ **Tell others your plan** and also tell them you are trying to overcome procrastination because it is robbing you, or at least threatening to slow you down, from the life you seek. Sharing with others will make your commitments firmer and allow the other person to reinforce your resolve.

❋ **Tasks that seem overwhelming can be broken up into small pieces.** It's easier to get started—then continue making progress—if you work on achievable chunks. Try to do the hardest task first thing in the morning, and you feel so good that you sail through many other tasks!

❋ **Get organized about how you want to proceed.** Make lists, set deadlines, and begin!

Poor Health

It is clear that a bad turn in your health or that of a loved one can be a Retirement Robber. When serious, chronic illness or disability strikes, it can become the focal point of time and energy, whether it is you or someone close to you. In this section, we look briefly at how to cope with and—importantly—how to prevent (as much as possible) these potential impediments to living a full life. **Chapter 8: Most Important of All: Your Health** covers prevention in more depth.

You can bring on a Retirement Robber by being in poor health or not taking care of yourself. It cannot be said strongly enough how important it is to stay in good shape physically and mentally. If you are in good shape, including exercising, eating healthily, and maintaining a positive mental attitude, you are less likely to fall ill or have long-term disabilities when an accident occurs. Accidents and the unexpected can happen.

Nancy can attest to this from an experience in 2013. She was jogging when a car hit her and sent her flying to a hard hit on the ground. Though she had several broken bones, she did not require surgery and recovered rather quickly. Even the doctors and physical therapists were impressed. No one doubted that it was due to her good physical condition and positive attitude, plus sheer luck and blessing not to have been injured worse. The outpouring of affection and help from family and friends added to recovery efforts, actually making it, on balance, a happy time. It turns out she was prepared for that whole incident without even realizing it.

You Can't Say No to Requests for Your Time

This is when your life is ruled by doing activities you don't really want to do. Sometimes people who are used to being workaholics might instinctively become volunteeraholics at first when they retire—that old feeling that a full schedule is a better one. We covered strategies for saying no earlier in this chapter.

You Want to Do it All

If you find yourself greatly fragmenting your time by engaging in so many activities that you are even busier than when you were working full-time and not really settling on a plan, you may be overindulging yourself. Yes, we have been suggesting you live the life you want, but after doing your dreaming and some experimenting, that means defining it and doing the planning. Perhaps you can set some deadlines for yourself to move forward.

Your Circle Goals also can help you plan. If you do your Circle Goals as best you can, you can assess your current activities against the plans and priorities you have outlined, including whether the activity contributes to or detracts from a balanced life.

Guilt

This human emotion can undermine your plans and confidence. Maybe you don't think you deserve to do what you have planned, to live the life you dream to live. You imagine that you could be using the resources or your talents in another way, perhaps accepting more of the requests for your time. You worry about those less fortunate than you who don't have the opportunity to do the types of things you are planning.

The truth is that you deserve your retirement and have earned this next chapter of your life. You have to give yourself permission to live the life you want and set your goals. If you serve all the causes that ask for your time, you will shortchange yourself. Some people turn their guilt into greater generosity in charitable giving or other positive acts.

Widowhood, Widowerhood, and Single Life

We've talked about external and internal Robbers. A category that stands apart as a potential Robber is not having a partner in life. Widowhood, widowerhood, and singlehood can be conditions that bring a whole range of emotions, actions, and reactions as regards one's retirement life. It can be a drawback, temporarily or permanently, or a chance to be free and entirely design your life your way.

Widowhood and Widowerhood

The death of a partner brings tremendous grief and sense of loss and interruption. At the same time, it can provide new opportunities for growth and exploration. Death after a long and difficult illness brings grief but can also be a relief. Each person perceives widowerhood or widowhood in his or her unique way. And it probably changes as time goes on and life's natural transitions take place.

Moving Ahead

Constance talks about when she first became a widow and says widowhood can be a Retirement Robber—if you let it be. Here is her voice:

> *"What do you do when you had all the dreams and plans with another person? When your friends are mostly couples? When your children are grown up and married and living far away? I think you have to work through the loss and grief and begin to reimagine your life. You have to reach down and reach out.*
>
> *"Time begins to heal, but time also stretches ahead, and you realize that you have time for new chapters of your life. It can be exhilarating. It doesn't have to be just as you planned with your husband. You are freer and more independent, just by virtue of being single. I love doing the things Thomas and I did together, and I have found new ways to enjoy them without him."*

Like Constance, you can build on the marriage legacy as well as construct a new story with new or old themes. You can continue a hobby that was shared, be it fishing or refinishing furniture or art collecting or cooking. You may want a new angle on it, such as trying new venues or styles.

What is your situation? Do you have a beloved pastime you shared with your spouse and want to continue? Something you can build on and make your own in a new way? Or maybe you both loved traveling overseas. What about volunteering overseas? You could do it with a friend. What about planning special annual trips individually with nieces and nephews? Maybe your spouse was allergic to dogs. What about adopting a shelter dog or two?

Or you can start something entirely new, as Loretta did with photography and ballroom dancing.

> *Loretta has such resilience. After 10 years as a widow, she still misses Van and lives in the home where she has lived for many years. She has built a very full life, with volunteer activities and several new passions. Children and grandchildren remain at the top of the list, as well as her elderly mother and many friends. She also has taken up photography and ballroom dancing, both quite seriously. These photographic and dancing activities are a joy.*

If you have had a professional career, does it take on a larger role now without your spouse? It is still important to you and undoubtedly provides substance and ongoing connection to your life, as well as a set of friends and contacts. This is a consideration in deciding when to retire, but remember that you can develop a whole new chapter with new interests, friends, and contacts.

Having a strong separate self is even more important. Some widows have had their identity so tied up with their husbands that they didn't know, at least initially, how to imagine or build a vibrant next chapter. Some have let it rob them, at least temporarily of the robust future they could have, such as by leaving their neighborhood and circle of friends earlier than necessary to go to a retirement home. Surely one can find new friends and a new way of life there, but it is good to take time to assess after a death, to ensure that is a good path. It may be just the right thing, or it may be too limiting at your age.

> *Gerry and Darlene had moved into a retirement community. When Gerry died, Darlene was lonely in spite of the interesting people with whom she now lived, and wondered if she should move back*

near her friends. She decided not to move but spends one night a week in the city with a friend so she can stay connected with her other friends. It works well for her.

As for other aspects of planning retirement, Constance's observation that you have to reach down and reach out is good advice. You cannot stand still. You have to move ahead with defining yourself and your dreams and putting the dreams in place.

Don's mother died after a struggle with Alzheimer's. It was so sad for Don's dad, Chet. He felt he had lost out on their "golden years." It had been like a promise that had slipped away as she grew more ill, and now that time together was gone. Chet loved golf and got back into playing often, which is where he met Donna, a widow. They started dating and are now so happy together. They travel, cook together, share several common interests, and of course play golf as often as possible. Now they are looking ahead at their golden years together.

Single Life

You may want a companion or you may not. For some people, single-hood and life without a significant other saps their retirement life because of having no built-in companion. For others, the independence is a great opportunity as full-time working life takes its place in the rearview window. The opportunity is to plan and move ahead unencumbered, being able to do what *you* want.

Every time we see Kathryn, she has a great smile on her face. She retired from her career and has a whole new life, especially after completing a 12-step program. She's single and loves it.

I've got a great circle of friends of all ages, both men and women. I travel lots in the U.S. and abroad. My new interests include my book club and a little business I started in editing and web design. A huge part of my life is mentoring several young women on an ongoing basis. I love this e.e. Cummings quote: 'It takes courage to grow up and turn out to be who you really are.' My life is happy, joyous, and free.

One often becomes more creative if planning alone. Anything goes. Think outside the box about travel and classes and other opportunities, and decide if you want to go alone or with a friend. There are so many opportunities and resources, many of which are covered in **Chapter 5: What Will I Do With My Time?** and the Appendix. Some examples are *www.backroads.com* for outdoor adventures, *www.abercrombiekent.com* for luxury trips, and just any exploration online of the activities you seek.

Seeking Companionship

Whether you are widowed or single for other reasons, you may want a companion to share your interests and life with you, or even to share fun events from time to time. The extent to which that person is a factor in or involved in planning your retirement chapter is up to you. And of course the situation can evolve as a relationship becomes more serious. If so, you will want to consult **Chapter 7: Renegotiating at Home** to learn more about the partnership aspects of retirement.

But how do you find someone? Talk to friends about dating and ease into it. Be in charge so outcomes are what you want.

If you want to meet someone for companionship or a romantic relationship, or want to find new friends, there are so many places to meet people. For example, you can go to reunions, alumni events, or on university trips. Stories abound about people who reconnected with a former boyfriend or girlfriend (or someone else) at a reunion—or on Facebook, as Arthur tells us:

> *"Ivy and I knew each other when we were 17. At that time she was dating my best friend from high school. Once we graduated, Ivy and I lost contact for nearly 40 years until 2009, when on a whim I found her on Facebook and contacted her. E-mails led to phone calls led to weekend visits. A year later, I moved into her place. In 2011 we were married."*

Many people enjoy "meetups," which are groups they find online to go to movies, lectures, dance lessons, hiking, and more. The groups self-form—you find them online and sign up to be notified—and you can get on the e-mail list and always know what's coming up. You can attend or not, as you wish. Maybe you will meet someone at the gym or as you engage in a sport. Look for local groups that do hikes around or near the city. You can join an interest club, like a book club, or engage in church activities.

And, of course, there is online dating, which is gaining in popularity in our age group. Consult with friends about the sites they like or about which they've heard good reviews. Be cautious, but do go out and enjoy meeting someone new in person after meeting online and chatting for a while. You may make a new friend, learn something about yourself, or even find that special someone.

Bottom line: Singlehood, widowhood, and widowerhood do not have to be Retirement Robbers, because you have choices.

 Exercise 6-1: Dealing with Retirement Robbers

Write five potential requests you think you might get from friends, family, nonprofits, etc. and think about whether each would be a Retirement Robber.

☐ Write how you would approach/respond to each of these requests.

CHAPTER 7

Renegotiating Life at Home

I married you for life, not lunch, but I do love you.

—Anonymous

If you have a spouse or partner or significant other with whom you live, this is for you. That person is a crucial part of the new life you are planning. Simply put, you will be sharing it. And you already know how important it is for things to go right at home, especially in times of change. You both need to be happy, but what happens when you are competing for the same space or gritting your teeth over a habit that is magnified by being together 24/7? This chapter is designed to flag some of the issues that can arise when one, or both, parties "retire," including the situation when one person is already retired or has been home full-time. Expectations can differ.

We explore the issues with which couples struggle and suggest some ways to cope with these transitions. Much of this also applies if you are living with friends. Our light-hearted shorthand for this chapter is *Whose kitchen is this, anyway?* or the quote above from someone who didn't want to be expected to prepare lunch every day for a newly retired husband. She has her own schedule! A preview of the advice we will offer can be summed up in three words: *communicate, communicate, communicate.*

And, we know that some of you are thinking of another word: *patience.* Yes, that too. Hopefully other words are excitement, re-engagement, and joy! Let's start with those.

Rediscovery

What a joy to rediscover one's couplehood! We know so many examples of people leaping into this new time of life together and forging ever-stronger bonds. They discover through more time together the traits and interests that brought them together. It can be even better if they explore new paths together, such as new kinds of travel or volunteer work or hobbies. This should be a great time of life for the two of you. You can rediscover each other and your relationship, plus figure out how to live together in a new way.

> *Phil and Bonnie, married for many years, retired within a few months of each other and knew they needed to downsize. They bought a small apartment in Boston and settled in. What fun they have! They have circles of friends together and separately. They spend time with their children and grandchildren. Travel is a priority. Was it an adjustment going from work to a small home with so much time together? Yes, they say, but they couldn't be happier because they believe in enjoying it all as a couple, yet they are conscious of needing to give each other space. No separate fiefdoms here!*

Sometimes just spending more time together as new routines get set is really special and increases the bonds.

> *Patty and Craig, happily married for more than 40 years and now retired, have their separate activities, but they nearly always have lunch and dinner together—because they want to, not because either demands it. If they don't have their meals together, it isn't a big deal, but they do find it a wonderful way to stay in sync and caught up on each other's interests, as well as to explore new ideas, like planning their next trip.*

Romance and special times together are important, too. If you had a date night every week or month while you were working, that is a great tradition to continue. Or you can start it now. Special time together outside the daily routine keeps life interesting and strengthens relationships.

This new chapter is also a time to treasure each other and watch out for each other's well-being. You are each other's best friend and keeper at this stage and, most likely, increasingly as you both age. Besides enjoying each other's company, you can help each other by watching for what can go wrong, such as signs of ill health or changes that could have health implications, including disrupted sleep patterns, marked memory change, striking energy level variation, or signs of depression.

Preparing

When a major transition like retirement enters your family, it is important to be thoughtful and sensitive to each other, communicate, and plan. Without that, each of you might make assumptions that create tensions in the relationship. Asking oneself and one's partner about hopes and dreams—and possible snafus!—at home is the best start, followed by planning the pathway together.

To start the discussion, you could each write down your ideal retirement day and compare as a way to see the differences. Then, put some of these questions on the table:

*   If one of us is already retired and in a routine at home, what will the changes be at home as the other person also retires? Or what will be the changes if we are retiring together?

*   Should space be divided up differently in the house?

*   What are our separate interests, and what do we like to do together?

*   What are our separate passions and "bucket list" goals?

*   How will all that come together in our life, and, particularly, how will it affect life at home?

*   Are our energy levels the same?

*   What if we don't have social networks after leaving work?

*   Who manages the finances and other matters at home? Will it change?

*   How can we solve issues that arise?

With your initial thoughts and discussion on some of these questions—or just having these questions in mind, it's time to move on to discuss some of the common issues that arise.

Sharing Space With Each Other: Territoriality

You share the living space with your significant other, and that can get tricky when life changes by one or both of you leaving a full-time career and spending more time at home. How that space is allocated, organized, and used becomes a key factor in a smooth transition and peace at home.

Whose kitchen is this, anyway? You may be thinking that as your spouse is suddenly home more and wants to reorganize the kitchen and start cooking again. Or your spouse may be saying that to you, as you come home and swoop in to take a more major role in cooking now that you have time. Have you discussed it?

And what about your office space? Most likely, you both use a computer and need desk space. And you both probably want privacy for a getaway place and to communicate.

Space allocation goes for other parts of the house, too. You always have shared while working, but the dynamics are bound to change with more time at home. You may want change or your spouse may. The space is the same but the day is different. *Where do we read the paper? I like that place on the couch. Why is the dining room table always cluttered now with your laptop and papers, when it used to look so nice with the wood showing, and it was so useful for our meals? Why is the TV suddenly on all the time, interrupting the silence I love so much? Or, worse, why do you have to have a TV on in every room?*

Another type of territoriality is reflected in the following story of Janice and Aaron, when he came home and staked out the territory of home maintenance.

> *Janice is a photographer and has long worked out of the home she shares with her husband, Aaron. When he retired and was home more, Aaron started second-guessing Janice's house maintenance, tearing apart the plumbing and slowly (took four months) putting it*

back. It nearly drove Janice crazy, and she says—only partly in jest, "Aaron needs a job to keep me sane!" Thankfully, he found other interests and has left the plumbing alone.

Some of the situations may be a bit comical; others not. The key is to talk about it rather than letting it simmer. You can work out an accommodation, especially now that you have more time to do so! Gentle requests coupled with solutions are a good start. For example: *I am now going to use the sewing machine I haven't used for twenty years, so what would you think about moving your books and fishing tackle off that table? There is room in the spare bedroom. And we need to plan ahead to set up an additional computer and desk space so we each have our own.*

Shelly has looked outside the home for a solution.

> *Both writers, Shelly and Alejandro live in a one-bedroom apartment. Shelly has developed a strategy of finding beautiful places around her neighborhood where she can go to write, such as a special coffee shop or park, and also places to take a break, including free afternoon concerts at the Juilliard School.*

Togetherness?

Togetherness is wonderful, and now you will have more time to be together than at any time since before you had children, or maybe since your career took off. Your routine will be changing, and most likely you now are coming into a time for becoming reacquainted with each other and the things you like to do together.

You have more time for your relationship, and, in theory, it should be a benefit. If your relationship is a good one that is working pretty well, it is likely to work even better as the two of you build your next chapter together. If the relationship has had difficulties, retirement and the closeness of the home quarters may aggravate the problems. Some marriages or close relationships cannot withstand the reintroduction to each other and the closer quarters of retirement. You don't want that to be yours!

When One Spouse Has More Need for Togetherness

As mentioned in **Chapter 6: Retirement Robbers and Other Challenges,** a number of people have told us that the biggest problem at home (a Retirement Robber) is a spouse who seems to be needy and underfoot. That may sound harsh, but an uneven situation in terms of time expectations can be draining. You can feel trapped if your partner expects you to be home and attentive all the time and depends on you totally for social interaction. These issues are dependence and possessiveness.

Dependence

A newly retired spouse may not have planned ahead in terms of social structure and activities, either not thinking in advance or not facing up to what retirement would look like. Such cases can place a greater burden on the other partner to be the constant source of activity both in the home and outside. It can be very stressful.

Carolyn has been retired from teaching for several years. Her husband, Stan, just retired, after traveling for his job all week every week. He was only in town on weekends and mainly did projects at home and never built friendships in the neighborhood or around town. He is dependent on her and expects her to spend all her time with him. She can get little else done and has had less time for her friends and the other activities she's enjoyed over the last few years. Her fear is that Stan won't make friends and will just continue to depend on her. He knows he's upset her routine but still depends on her.

I Want You All to Myself!

Sometimes one part of the couple has retired earlier or had a career in the home and that person has been waiting patiently (or not) for the partner to retire. The one at home may envision unlimited time together going forward, sort of an ownership of the other person's time. That may work or not, but it is important to realize that each of you will have goals and expectations that must be discussed. You are still two individuals with demands on each other as a couple but also with your own separate wants, needs, and agendas.

Joanie had waited for three years after leaving her career for Dixon to retire. Now was the time together they had talked about for so long! Every meal, daily activities, she thought. Working in the garden together. At last he was home! However, he thought of it as a time to be together but also for him to improve his golf game (she didn't play), renew old friendships, and read lots of books. Their vision of the day and level of togetherness differed dramatically, exacerbated by Joanie's persistent view that Dixon was now retired and home to be with her. She didn't want to share him.

What to Do

The situations in the stories above are ripe for planning and communicating. We would suggest that the couples do some joint visioning and planning regarding their activities together and separately. They could find new activities together, which could lead to meeting new friends. Carolyn and Dixon can stress how important their separate activities are to their happiness, and they can encourage their spouses to explore some new interests or revive old ones. They might want to make concrete suggestions of possible new interests and ideas on how to start out.

What if this happens to you, and your spouse doesn't agree with your suggestions? This is the perfect time for better communication, including really listening. The more you take into account each other's desires, even those subtly set forth, the more the two of you can be in sync in figuring out your together and separate time. It's a process of exploration and may take some time.

Balance Between Togetherness and Your Own Life

We use the word *balance* because we believe each half of the partnership has to have individual interests—hobbies, pastimes, continuing work. You will share much in your lives, including perhaps hobbies plus day-to-day activities and special circumstances, such as travel and time with the grandchildren. Some couples even start businesses together. However, you need to be able to pursue what interests you, and it may not be the same as what interests your partner. He likes the symphony and you don't. Fine, he can go with a friend. She likes tennis and you don't. Fine, you can go to the gym—and then read for your book club. Separate activities keep both parties fresh and interesting, contributing to the richness of your time together.

Each person also needs time alone. Time alone is crucial to any human being. You need to have your own space in order to enjoy time with others. Whether it is reading the paper or walking alone, meditating, reading a book, or exercising, the time benefits you. You can think, learn, refresh, and reenergize.

Janey goes to yoga five mornings a week. Walking there along city streets in every season, the calming yoga practice, and a cup of tea afterward are great nourishment for her. Chester, on the other hand, likes to read the newspaper and take a long walk to greet the day. When they return home, they are ready to participate in the day they've planned, whether together or with more time alone.

Time and Expectations

Retired couples often have general ideas of exciting things they will do together, such as travel, but they may not have considered how it will go in day-to-day life.

Daily Life

The routine of being at home together may be the main feature of life—or at least the one that has to be figured out. Perspectives may differ radically. Picture the husband or wife who has been at home and on an independent schedule suddenly confronted by his or her partner wanting to have lunch prepared every day. And right at noon, please! Another expectation may be that one partner will be the social secretary of the other. This may not go over well, when one takes into account the hours of logistical planning.

Other issues arise, too: *Will the apportionment of chores change (shopping, bill paying, care of the cars)? Will we both cook now? Will we give up the house cleaner? Will more home responsibilities fall on one rather than the other? Do we have the same energy levels and how does that impact our life?*

These are all questions to be anticipated and talked about in advance. Even talking about them without precisely solving them is good because you become aware of issues that can arise.

Honey-Do's

One issue is "honey-do's"—you know, the lists that one spouse hands another of all the tasks that need to be done around the house. More open time can lead to long and quite interesting lists! *Please clean the gutters and retile the bathroom and fix the doorknob. Let's plant a vegetable garden. Let's clean the attic. Let's go through everything we have in storage.* Often the "let's" is not so much "let us" but "why don't you." It's good to be sensitive to how much is being asked. Maybe hiring or retaining the handyman is actually a good idea. And many of the projects really do need to be done together.

> *After a formal retirement and a special trip, Tony and his wife settled into life at home. Tony had always thought he would do some form of work after retirement, and indeed he found out that total retirement wasn't his cup of tea. "I missed working. So, I found a great job!" Of course, he also told us in some jest that "the tasks at home were getting more difficult, and I just didn't want to be climbing up and down ladders and doing that kind of thing." He now is able to spend more time at home than before he "retired," very much enjoying the time with his wife rather than filling it up with onerous tasks that they now hire someone else to do.*

Who's in Charge?

Another issue is "Who's in charge?" One or both of you may be used to being in charge at work—or being fully in charge at home. Retirement brings changed circumstances and may require an attitude adjustment!

> *Darren was the CEO of a large global advertising firm. Upon Darren's retirement, his wife found that Darren was giving her orders and tasks to do and was simply in her hair. After a few weeks, she declared one day, "You may have been the CEO of a large, successful company, but you are not CEO of this home." Darren stopped delegating and making so many demands and instead started to think of their home as a shared responsibility.*

Communicating

It all comes down to communicating about expectations and what is working or not. The expectations of one spouse for the other have to be discussed and carefully considered. The two visions need to be on the same track.

As Darren's wife figured out, she had to put her foot down when Darren's unconscious bossiness threatened their tranquility. She made her statement, and Darren took heed. In the case of Tony, he self-selected out of the honey-do's that didn't fit his new lifestyle. He and his wife worked out that he would go back to work, and they would pay for certain tasks to be accomplished at home.

In both cases, talking and making one's position clear were key. When you do it, it may take several discussions and explorations together to get the issues on the table and deal with them. Being forthright is the best policy, but also be willing to compromise and look for solutions together.

When the Two of You Are Not Alone

Your living situation may include more than just the two of you. As a member of the sandwich generation, you may have parents, children, or other relatives in your home. Multigenerational living is on the rise, especially as trends of job loss and unemployment and pressures on Social Security and healthcare push people out of independent living.

These multigenerational situations can be challenging and create additional stress on your couplehood, as more people are now home more of the day, and vying for the same space and your attention. There are inevitably privacy issues, too. **Chapter 3: Making Your Money Last** and **Chapter 6: Retirement Robbers and Other Challenges** cover some of the issues and possible approaches regarding finances and setting boundaries for when the kids come back home to live. This section focuses more on older relatives living with you, and **Chapter 8: Most Important of All: Your Health** has more on their health and insurance.

Another type of living situation is when two or more couples share a house or when a couple rents part of the house out. The issues of space, privacy, and inclusion will almost certainly crop up.

Space and Time

The book *All in the Family: A Practical Guide to Successful Multigenerational Living* by Sharon Graham Niederhaus and John L. Graham is one great resource for this situation. Among other things, it discusses the dynamics as well as solutions. It is not possible for everyone to build extra entrances and kitchens, but allocation of space and remodeling can ease competition over space.

The traditional "mother-in-law suite" can be a godsend. It is a bedroom/bathroom space, perhaps with a small kitchen, where the parent, relative, or adult child can be independent. Some people now are building these spaces—sometimes called "granny flats"—by expanding their homes, building a new small structure on their property, or reallocating space. The book *In-Laws, Outlaws, and Granny Flats* by Michael Litchfield is full of ideas and specifics on how to create granny flats to meet multigenerational living challenges with common sense, creativity, and compassion.

Family togetherness need not be total. You as a couple can spend time alone—and you should. You may choose to eat out with friends and not invite your parents or kids. All parties need to have independent lives, as much as physical capacity allows, but even a homebound person will need separate friends and times to get together without the whole family.

Caregiving

When your parent lives with you, it may be—or develop into—a case of caregiving, which can be both a joy and a burden in the home. You may need to adapt the home space through construction or other means to make it senior-appropriate. You will have additional responsibilities that take much of your time. And it will affect the whole family in terms of space, time, and privacy. We are not arguing against it, but rather saying to be aware of the impact and requirements. For example, if you are the caretaker at home, you will have extra stress and must watch out for yourself so you stay strong. This includes accepting offers of help and going out with friends for lunch or taking a long walk, having outside interests, and finding support spiritually.

We find Mike's family's story instructive on multiple aspects of having an older parent in the home:

Mike's dad, Duane, was in his 80s when he moved in with Mike's sister Barbara and her husband, Gregg. Duane moved into the master suite on the main floor, while Barbara and Gregg moved upstairs. They began senior-proofing the house, including modifications to the bathroom, such as a seat in the shower and non-slip tile. Barbara's siblings urged her to hire in-home help, which Duane could afford, but she wanted to do it herself and retired from her job to do so.

Barbara remembers with pleasure having her dad in the house, even though it was a considerable adjustment for all, including the two teenage daughters, for whom it was a loss of some space and privacy and ease of bringing friends home. It was especially a challenge for all when Duane would get up at 2 a.m. and begin rustling—well, really, banging and crashing—around in the kitchen to make a snack. And he sometimes left the burner on when he finally retired to bed, causing further consternation—but not as much consternation and bedlam as when sometimes the fire alarm would go off in the middle of the night!

After about two years, Duane fell in the shower and broke his hip, necessitating hospital and rehab care. All agreed it was time for assisted living, where he lived out his days, with frequent visits from his family.

Mike's reflection from this experience with his dad, siblings, and Barbara's immediate family is that one's parents are always further along in aging than you want to think or are willing to admit. You may not be ready for the next step they need—such as assisted living—but that may be what they need.

Every story is individual. Some people can't afford assisted living or any kind of care outside the home. Others do use in-home care. Certainly not everyone wants to or can afford to remodel or build new spaces. These are all family decisions that lend themselves well to lots of fact-gathering, information-sharing, and discussions in family meetings, as well as e-mail.

 Exercise 7-1: What Are the Home Issues?

Think about the issues that have arisen or could arise between you and your spouse related to life at home after retirement.

☐ Jot down a list and have a discussion with your spouse, clarifying the issues and seeking input and ideas about how the two of you will handle the issues now and in the future.

CHAPTER 8

Most Important of All:
Your Health

The greatest wealth is health.

—Virgil

Here's our message on health: *Now is the time to revolutionize your health. There is no better time and no greater priority for you.* We know you want to live a healthy and active life, and that means staying in shape and practicing prevention to avoid chronic disease. You know what to do; advice and information are published or pronounced for us in media every day. The challenge is to do it, whether it is easy or hard for you. Become empowered.

Now, lowering the decibel level a little: Your health is your most precious asset, and good health is the surest ticket to vibrant next chapters of your life. When you don't have your health, it can be all you think about; it can be all-consuming. As you get ready for or start retirement, you can reinvent your health by proactively investing in maintaining and improving it. You can try new health strategies to rebuild or strengthen your health for the exciting time ahead. Preventive health activities need to begin to take more of your time.

This chapter is about investing in your health for now and the future. It's about the tools for your health. We discuss many aspects, from best practices in maintaining physical, mental, and spiritual health to being proactive in looking ahead to your needs and what can change with your health. We also cover health planning, including some aging considerations for your parents and other loved ones and you.

Plan for Your Health for Now and the Future

Good health can neither be assumed nor ignored. The costs of not managing health can overshadow and decrease quality of life. Yes, we all will face health issues, because that is part of life. Many already face some of those issues. Although you can't know everything about your future and what course your health will take, you can anticipate and plan ahead for life's progression. We know so many people who are doing well in their 80s and 90s, even after illnesses. What an inspiration to us all, just being aware that, with care, our bodies can carry us through illness and back to health.

Unless you already have a chronic illness, we would guess that you envision your next stage of life as featuring the current, healthy *you*. That's a good way to start. The key is to keep it that way, as well as to be realistic about your current state of health, what can change, and what plans need to be put in place for those changes.

Or, you may be one of many who are leaving your full-time work in a very stressed-out state—stressed, burned out, and perhaps overweight. You need personal reinvigoration and something of a health makeover.

We have to work to attain and maintain good health when we encounter accidents or other physical problems and as we age. It is wise to plan activities at different ages that are compatible with the likely health of that age. Climb mountains? Sure, but maybe not after a certain age. Run marathons? Sure, as long as you can, but probably not after a certain age—although we know people in their 60s and 70s who are still running! Keep jogging, or switch to a walk/run. *Walk every day.* All your life. It's one of the healthiest things you can do. Play tennis as long as you can: singles now, doubles later. Ski downhill vigorously now, cross-country later. Take vacations with rigorous physical activities now. Do yoga into your 90s and beyond. There are more and more people living past 100, more so than at any other time in history, and one of their secrets is that they have stayed active physically. Carl, now 101, played doubles tennis into his mid-80s.

We can't predict our health with clarity. We certainly can learn about potential problems to which we will be most vulnerable (through genetics and testing), but we cannot know for certain what will happen. We also can watch the progression of others as they age and/or deal with illness, and we can read studies or articles. This provides knowledge about normal aging, chronic illness, and what else can happen. Knowledge provides room to anticipate and plan. And the inspiring stories of others can lead us forward.

Rita's Story

Rita's story is one of being in shape physically and mentally before major illness struck. She received a cancer diagnosis in late 2010. Barely missing a beat, she had surgery and radiation. A year later, she had a recurrence and chemotherapy was prescribed.

Throughout, Rita has kept up her schedule, including lots of travel in the United States and abroad. She's indefatigable and optimistic. It must be hard at times, but she does it. She says she plans the travel to have something to look forward to between chemo sessions and rounds. Here's what else Rita says:

> *Being diagnosed with cancer was a shock. I thought I was on top of my game. But, being in shape physically and mentally before a sudden illness was exactly what has enabled me to get through treatments and to continue to live a full and rich life. I miss active sports, but still make yoga, Pilates, Gyrokenisis, Qi Gong, stretching, and walking a priority. I eat mostly vegetables and have cut out sugar and dairy. To support my spirit, I journal daily, listen to meditation tapes and wonderful music, and am blessed to have a wide support network of wonderful friends. When you live with cancer, you value every day and every little thing in life, and therefore I need good health.*

Staying Healthy: Take Charge and Do it Now

Physical, mental, and spiritual are all components of a holistic approach to health, an approach that can be quite proactive and even aggressive. By aggressive, we mean pushing it. But here's the secret: By pushing it initially, it becomes a habit and an ingrained part of the lifestyle, and creates a pattern in your brain that becomes a habit over time.

Start with a physical, and then have a physical every year. Medicare offers a free physical as soon as you become eligible for Medicare. Medicare also covers bone density, mammogram, colonoscopy, PSA, and other tests, so get those at a minimum. Have your hearing checked, too, because if you don't take care of this early enough, the nerve endings can deteriorate.

Then address any health issues. Do any necessary additional tests. If you have a medical condition, figure out how to address it; and get a second opinion, if you can, on serious matters. If you can't get an appointment at the best place or the place of your choice for a second opinion or treatment, this is the time to use your network.

Perhaps you'd like to follow a strategy that Mike and Norinne have adopted. Every five years they go to the Mayo Clinic in Scottsdale, Arizona, for overall checkups, which gives them peace of mind. Comprehensive, holistic medical assessments can be effective in prevention and in helping to address ongoing issues.

You don't have to go to the Mayo Clinic. You can find other institutions, doctors, or advisors who can give you that comprehensive approach to your health. Look for people who try to find and treat root causes. Check the Appendix for resources.

If being overweight is the problem, get a plan and begin to lose weight. Obesity is an invitation to other diseases and can inhibit your ability to enjoy the kind of life you want to lead. No one has said it is easy, but it is important to start. A nutritionist and trainer can help.

If alcohol is the problem, Alcoholics Anonymous has been the answer for so many.

When drugs are prescribed, it is okay—even important—to ask if there are non-drug alternatives, such as exercise or nutrients or a different diet versus blood pressure medicine. It won't always be possible, but it is at least good to ask. A nutritionist may be able to reduce medications. Sometimes it's a matter of trying non-drug therapy for a while before going on the medication. As people age, they are prescribed more and more medications. It's important to stay on top of that, know the purpose of each, and be certain that all your doctors know all the medications you are taking.

For a holistic view, you can go to the Website of the American Society of Consulting Pharmacists (*www.ascp.com/find-senior-care-pharmacist*) to find a trained pharmacist to consult about your medicines and conditions.

Attitude is a big part of health. Having a healthy, realistic, and aware view of your health can lead to a better life. If you are aware of problems or a behavior (like smoking) or controllable condition that could limit this special time of life, why would you not address it and try to limit its impact? Living with a chronic disease is not fun!

You can start building your Health Team of Experts here: your primary doctor, any specialists, maybe a nutritionist, an integrative medicine doctor or institute. You also may be interested in health newsletters. For example, Denise Austin offers a newsletter of health tips (sign up at *www. deniseaustin.com/newsletter-signup*) and a full Website with exercises and other assistance, and there are many other valuable general and issue-focused health newsletters of major clinics, hospitals, and authorities. See the Appendix for resources for both women and men, including *www.belvoir.com/titles/index.html for a list.*

Healthy Eating

A health advocate told us, "With what you put on your fork, you choose to be healthier or less healthy. You can choose healthier." But, you may first need to sort out what is best for you. If you have health issues, including being overweight, it's good to speak with your doctor. You will see article upon article of advice in every media form. You probably know what to do, but here are some reminders:

* **Eat in moderation** and enjoy the food as you eat.

* **Eat smaller portions.** For example, a main-course serving of fish or poultry should be the size of your palm. Some people use a smaller plate so it looks like more food. Why not buy a gorgeous or fun plate and do that? You can use a nice placemat and sit down to eat.

* **Eat something every five hours** so you do not get hungry and gorge. Have healthy snacks handy: hummus, blueberries, air-popped popcorn, a handful of almonds, one stick of string cheese, an apple.

* **Eat a balanced diet** of lean protein, fruits and vegetables, dairy, and whole-grain carbs. You need all of them, though sometimes a special diet will cut an element. Err on the side of more fruits and vegetables, as they are full of nutrition. Think colors: Lots of leafy greens and berries are great antioxidants. Fish such as salmon and sardines are super for you because of the fish oil (omega-3).

* **Drink water** every time you think of it throughout the day, starting first thing in the morning. This also fills you up before meals and helps with losing weight.

* **Do not eat sugar.** It can lead to major disease (including possibly Alzheimer's) and, of course, more weight. If you do eat sweets, use natural sources of sugar, such as honey or maple syrup. And stay away from soda drinks!

* **Avoid deep-frying and use non-saturated oils,** such as canola and olive, for cooking and salad dressing.

* **And did we mention that a glass of red wine is actually good for you?**

You can track calories, at least for a while, to see how you are doing, whether trying to maintain your weight or lose some. Many people find online sites and smartphone apps really handy for this. The MyFitnessPal app helps with calorie counting and encouragement.

Physical Health: Staying in Shape

We need not belabor here the benefits of staying in good physical shape. It is natural, smart advice with observable benefits. People who are couch potatoes or obese are more likely to live shorter lives and develop some illnesses sooner than people with an active lifestyle. Balance is an issue, too, as we age and can fall. Simple exercises can help. So, it is beneficial to take small steps every day that are part of a healthy lifestyle, as well as the larger steps. What does that mean? Read below for our advice, gleaned and collated from numerous professional and practical sources, many of which are in the Appendix of this book.

Exercise—Body

You can start with everyday activities, like routinely taking the stairs a couple flights instead of the elevator. Park the car a few blocks from your destination and walk.

Walk to work or the store a longer way every few days, or every day.

You can have a hobby that involves exercise, such as shooting hoops or playing golf. The beauty of golf is that it can be played into later decades of life.

> *Bob's parents are both 89, and they love to golf. It's a sport they took up after retirement. They used to travel to different golf courses, even overseas, but now mainly play at their local club in Virginia. Do they use a golf cart? No. They prefer to walk, saying that's great for their health.*

Walking

Walking may be the best. Studies show that walking regularly can dramatically decrease risk of cancer, high blood pressure, initial heart attacks, development of diabetes, and strokes. It's free and available. Put on a pair of tennis shoes and walk out the door. Take a walk after dinner or walk early every morning. Or get to the shopping mall and walk around in there, as so many people do, especially in bad weather.

Walking is a great social exercise. So many people enjoy pairing up to walk and talk. We've met people who have done this for years. Exercise is quite often easier with a pal as inspiration and insistence. It's harder to stay in bed and skip walking when your neighbor is waiting for you!

Another type of pal for walking is a pedometer, a little device that tracks the steps and distance you walk in a day. You may be surprised at how it all adds up, especially if you set a goal like the 10,000 steps a day as recommended by a former U.S. Surgeon General. We have pedometer suggestions in the Appendix.

Variety

Exercise possibilities are endless. Nancy does a run/walk along the Potomac River in Washington, DC. It's 35 minutes two or three times a week, and it gives her a solid sense of accomplishment. It's even better when she adds 10–15 minutes of 5- to 10-pound weights after the run, and has a trainer for strength training twice a week. Others do much more. Just do what you want to and try to push for several times a week. Compete with yourself, not that friend who can heft 40 pounds. If you can exercise for 30 minutes a day five or six days a week, you are really at the top of your game, but don't do the muscle exercises (except abs) two days in a row, as muscles need time to rest and recoup. Do employ interval training, which is short bursts of intensity.

Exercise everywhere! Outdoor exercise is fun and can take so many forms, including hiking, biking, climbing, volleyball, golf, kayaking, swimming, and more. It's fun to learn by tagging along with a friend. Our friend Jan found swimming as a lifelong sport by doing that. Your exercise friends would be part of your Health Team of Experts. Plus you also might want a trainer.

For indoor exercise, you also can join a gym, or you may live in a place that has a gym, thus avoiding the expense. And do take advantage of fitness centers and swimming pools when you stay at hotels. Always pack tennis shoes, a pair of shorts, and a swimming suit, and you are ready anytime! Some hotels offer gym clothes and shoes for rent.

Exercise at home. It doesn't have to cost a lot. Yes, you can buy major fitness equipment if you have the space and resources. More simply and still effectively, you can buy weights, a jump rope, latex bands, and maybe a yoga mat. Exercise videos and DVDs proliferate, and you can even find exercise routines on YouTube! Janie told us she feels like YouTube gives her a full gym in her living room, with all the classes she could want—and on her own schedule.

Do balance exercises all your life. Bones grow more fragile with age and doing balance exercises helps prevent falls, which are a major risk for older people. Simple, specific balance exercises available on the AARP Website (*www.aarp.org*) are so important. Some yoga poses and tai chi (discussed in more detail later) are enjoyable and effective in improving balance. We do a couple of minutes of balance exercises every morning, regardless of what other exercise we'll do during the day. They strengthen the core, too.

Find your fit. You don't have to go to the gym and suffer. Discover new ways to be healthy. The bottom line is to get into the habit of exercising, find an exercise form that you like, and change it up from time to time. Put it on your calendar. Reinvent into your own activity. It is critically important now to enjoying a healthy life, and it will make you physically stronger if and when you might have an injury or an illness.

Exercise–Brain Link

Brain health is as important as body health. We all stress over losing memory and, even worse, developing a debilitating brain disease like Alzheimer's or dementia. Some memory loss—those "senior moments" of forgetting a name or where you put the car keys—are normal and should not be cause for concern. On the other hand, it is true that Alzheimer's and dementia are on the rise. Some experts say that brain decline is not necessarily an inevitable part of aging (though there is a genetic component for some), and they recommend ways to be proactive about preventing these diseases and mitigating general brain decline.

One way is brain exercise. Now, you can go online or on a smartphone app and do daily brain exercises to strengthen memory, flexibility, attention, brain speed, problem-solving, and other aspects of brain function. Two popular Websites are Luminosity and AARP BrainHQ. More games and helpful articles can be found on the AARP Website (*www.aarp.org*).

Socialize regularly. A 2011 study that followed individuals now in their 80s for up to 12 years showed that people who are active with other people are half as likely to develop dementia or Alzheimer's as those with lower levels of social activity. The socializing stimulates the brain. This includes going out to restaurants, volunteering, sporting events, and any kind of activity enjoyed with others. We know groups of friends who go bird watching.

Activities that involve intellectual enjoyment are helpful, with someone or by yourself. When you go to a museum, learn a new language, read, or do crossword puzzles or Sudoku, you are stimulating your brain. The brain likes novelty and especially loves to learn new things. The effects are the creation of new neurons, increased effectiveness of brain area connections, and increased blood supply.

Eating healthily has a positive effect on brain health, and studies show certain foods can reduce the risk of Alzheimer's disease. Brain foods include fatty fish like salmon; walnuts and other nuts; antioxidants and flavonoids like blueberries, strawberries, pomegranate, and other fruit and vegetable juices; Brussels sprouts and broccoli; dried beans; folates like spinach and other dark leafy greens; curry powder/turmeric; and (drum roll) wine and dark chocolate. See the Appendix for a book by Isaacson and Ochner on diet to help prevent Alzheimer's, articles, and Websites.

Physical exercise, especially something aerobic like walking, is excellent. Weight training has been shown to improve memory. Moderate, or even more, exercise is the very best way to keep a healthy brain.

Depression can be something that creeps up on us. Exercise, dancing, listening to music, socializing, reading interesting books and watching movies, and many other activities can help ward off depression. What about giggles and gales of laughter with those grandchildren? Silliness can be a tonic. Staying in touch with friends is extremely important too. They reinforce you and help keep loneliness at bay.

Some of the best ways to stay in good mental and spiritual health are:

* **Friends and family.** These nurturing relationships remind us of who we have been during our lives and who we are now. Socializing is so uplifting to the spirit. And, we hardly need to mention the joy of being with grandchildren or young nieces and nephews.

* **Pets.** Animals, especially loving pets, are special in our lives. If you are lonely, you may want to adopt a pet, especially from an animal shelter. Or if you can't have pets where you live. See if a pet can visit. Also, volunteer at an animal shelter or to pet sit for friends.

* **Laughter.** Laughter has been scientifically proven to stimulate brain activity and also mood, helping emotional health and connection. Call up an old friend to reminisce, or watch a comedy, or think of a funny episode in your life when you laughed so hard you cried. And have you heard of laughter yoga in which people gather to add hearty laughter to their yoga poses?

* **Adult play.** San Antonio, Los Angeles, and Miami–Dade County in Florida are at the forefront of this trend. New York City built an adult playground in the Bronx and is building more due to its popularity. Think monkey bars, exercise equipment, and outdoor fitness stations in parks—for adults.

* **Journaling.** We suggest writing every morning in a journal. It's an excellent way to express your feelings and try out new ideas. You can blow off steam or dream.

✸ **Nature.** Does your spirit soar when you are out in nature or when you catch sight of a beautiful scene? If so, look for opportunities to be in nature, such as a walk in the park, a drive outside of town, a hike, or just stopping to drink in a spectacular sunset.

✸ **Art and music.** The powerful spirituality of art and music is undeniable. Both can lift one out of the everyday sameness or troubles and stimulate the mind. Groove on the music of your youth and all the memories it brings. Enjoy classical music or any music you love, along with ballet, opera, museums, and art gallery openings.

✸ **Dancing or other movement.** Moving to music, whether in exercise in a group or pair, quietly or enthusiastically, can spur well-being. Any kind of dancing from ballroom to rock to swing to western is just plain good for the soul. And the health benefits of moving and being happy go along with it.

✸ **Meditation.** Studies show that it can improve psychological well-being by reducing stress and anxiety. It can improve memory, critical thinking, and creativity. Physically, it reduces blood pressure and can boost the immune system. Meditating can be a challenge, so keep working at it, even for five minutes at a time and try to find a form that fits you to clear your mind from your daily "mental chatter." For example, you can take classes or use meditation CDs and videotapes.

✸ **Yoga and Pilates.** You can do yoga and Pilates at any age. They are legendary for their effect on body and mind health. Yoga has been credited with keeping the body limber and helping to maintain balance, and it can contribute to preventing shrinkage of the vertebrae (the bones of the spinal column).

✸ **Tai chi.** Many are turning to the gentle art of tai chi (or the simpler version called t'ai chi chih), an ancient Chinese exercise form that combines deep breathing and relaxation with slow, gentle movements. It can boost mental health, as well as improve balance and flexibility, thus reducing the risk of falls. It's great to reduce blood pressure too. See the AARP Website (*www.aarp.org*) for articles and exercises.

✸ **Sound and rhythm.** As a healing and stress-reducing practice, you can use any musical instrument you might play, such as drums, or Tibetan singing bowls, or crystal bowls. Because the body is made up of 80 percent water, the vibrations of sound affect our bodies positively and

157

reassuringly. Listening to music you love can get you up in the morning, motivate you during the day, and help you relax for sleep.

Other activities that take us outside of ourselves can increase spirituality and mental health, such as:

* **Giving back.** Volunteering can lift the spirit. Even though it may seem like an effort at first to find an opportunity and actually go do it, it can be a joy to make new connections and to see how you can help others.

* **Church or other.** Religion may provide just the spiritual support you need, and it also provides a social connection and community that can be sustaining and nurturing. Tradition can be wonderfully reassuring, and faith can be so comforting. Praying is a kind of meditation, and it is uplifting and life affirming for millions.

* **Gratitude.** If you start each day by saying aloud or writing what you are grateful for, you are more likely to be in a positive mood and more optimistic.

We do not mean to downplay depression with these suggestions. If you are feeling the effects of persistent depression, you should consult your physician. Some people do need medicine to help. Depression can be very serious. In particular, the recession that began in 2008 and difficulties accepting the realities of aging are contributing to a rise in suicides of Baby Boomers.

The Future

No Promises: Surprises Along the Way at Any Age

You can be in the best of health and living your life when something changes. It can be an accident or a surprise diagnosis. It can be a sudden heart attack or stroke. You can do everything right, and there are no promises. Richard never smoked or drank, ate healthily, and stayed in good shape. He was felled by melanoma at 67. Others live to 99 or longer.

There are surprises; we cannot know the future. Rita learned that when she received her cancer diagnosis. One day healthy, the next facing surgery, radiation, and chemotherapy. It happens to us and our friends and family. *It is always a surprise because we tend to think such health problems will skip us.* But the truth is that we nearly all will face health adversity one day. It may be a quick death at any age, or it may come at an early age and remain with us as a chronic illness, such as diabetes, cancer, and many other diseases including Alzheimer's. Or it may come when we are older. And, as older people know, it may be one thing after another. We are learning or have learned that with our parents.

> *Nancy's mother, Hildegarde, from Minnesota, was a code breaker in Washington, DC, during World War II. She was healthy until about age 67, when she developed breast cancer, which was cured after surgery. Then in 1997, she had open-heart surgery to replace a valve. Then that valve had to be replaced in 2004. She had pneumonia several times and back surgery. She has atrial fibrillation and is hard of hearing. At 91, she had surgery to install a cochlear ear implant, then three more surgeries because the wound didn't heal. Various events have moved her from independent living with her 100-year-old husband, Carl, to hospital to rehab and then to assisted living. She gets frustrated with low energy but mainly has a good attitude every day, including setting goals for herself. All her mental faculties are intact, as is her sense of humor—and her sense of reality. She already knows there have been and will be surprises.*

Healthcare Insurance and Medicare

Please be sure you have enough insurance. We are living longer, and diseases that used to kill people now can be managed, so health costs rise dramatically with age and longevity. Sadly, healthcare costs can soar to $266,000 per couple from age 65 to the end of their lives *in addition to what Medicare pays* and not including long-term care.

Know exactly what your health insurance covers by way of hospitals, rehab, and in-home care after the Medicare coverage runs out. Evaluate whether you've got enough insurance, or are paying too much for what you have. The Medicare phone help line can help you to understand what Medicare covers and at what point your supplemental coverage and long-term insurance need to step in. The supplemental can be pretty automatic, but long-term insurance must be specifically activated. Some people hesitate to use it until they are very old, for fear of using up the benefit. If you wait too long, you may not get its full benefit. Or if you use it up too early, you won't see the benefit later. It is tough to know what to do, but if you have the full picture of your resources and options, decisions can be made better. We provide a little more detail here and resources in the Appendix.

Medicare

Learn how Medicare works. You will receive an avalanche of documents the year before you are eligible, so do not worry about being left out. You will have Medicare at age 65 (unless that law changes) but will need additional health insurance and resources as you age. Be aware for your planning that you must pay for Medicare with a monthly premium that depends on your income level (from a little more than $100 to several hundred), and Medicare by itself only covers 80 percent of your medical expenses.

Supplemental Insurance and Drug Plans

You can add supplemental insurance and a drug plan as soon as you are Medicare-eligible to cover the 20 percent that Medicare does not cover. You will receive many offers and also can research your local options on the Medicare Website (*www.medicare.gov*). It works well. Many people can retain health insurance from their work as the supplemental. Some people wait to acquire (and thus pay for) the additional coverage because they have low medical expenses, but there is the risk that sudden medical surprises can incur high expenses that would not have adequate coverage. We know from experience that it takes lots of research and comparisons to figure this all out. It's good to talk to others who are sorting through the same process to compare notes and commiserate! Add a friend already on Medicare to your Health Team of Experts!

Long-Term Care Insurance

Consider long-term care insurance (LTC) as suggested in **Chapter 3: Making Your Money Last** for the time when you are running out of resources and for instances where the standard Medicare coverage has expired, normally 90 days. LTC covers in-home health care, nursing homes, and rehab facilities. It can be procured for different levels of coverage (for example, 50 percent or 100 percent), with the monthly premium being more costly for more extensive coverage. LTC is relatively expensive and becomes more expensive to procure as you age, so it is wise to research it earlier rather than later.

Medicaid

If you entirely run out of all your financial resources, you will be eligible for Medicaid. It is the last resort. The question is whether you want to exhaust all your assets to use it. With planning ahead, you are more likely to avoid this in your later years. One issue is the financial impact on a surviving spouse of depleting all your assets. Consulting an eldercare lawyer/specialist can help in addressing these situations.

Emergency Point of Contact

Designate your first choice "go-to" person in the event of an emergency and be certain that person knows where all your financial information is in case they need to do any work for you while you are recovering. Designate a backup person, too. And be sure both the primary and backup person know of their designated roles!

End-of-Life Planning and Documents

There are whole books and many experts you can consult on end-of-life planning. We mention here some of the key documents you will need and expand upon the living will on our Website. We recommend using a lawyer for drawing up and executing the first four documents listed. There are now Websites that help you manage all of the data and papers that you need to keep together, but it is advisable for your Team of Experts to include a lawyer and/or expert on eldercare.

Make decisions early, because you cannot predict when or how your physical or mental capacities will decline. Review the decisions and documents every couple of years.

Durable Power of Attorney

Durable powers of attorney enable you to have your affairs handled by a trusted person after you become incapacitated. You prepare the document and sign it while you are still capable, appointing another person to act for you as you. You execute such a document if you think you will not be able to make your own decisions at some point (which, really, could be all of us). At the time you sign it, you must know what the power of attorney does, to whom you are giving the power of attorney, and what property may be affected by it. The document can confer either general power or power in certain limited circumstances. Common powers include signing papers, checks, title documents, contracts, handling bank accounts, and other activities in the name of the person granting the power. More specific powers exist, such as to execute real estate documents.

The power of attorney is effective as soon as you sign it, unless you state that it is only to be effective upon the happening of some future event. The most common occurrence states that the power of attorney will become effective only if and when you (the signer) become disabled, incapacitated, or incompetent.

Durable Power of Attorney for Healthcare

In this document, you appoint a healthcare agent, or healthcare proxy, as someone you choose to make healthcare decisions for you when you cannot. This person will act only when you are not able to. You also may appoint a backup person.

Will

You need to have a will. Formally called a last will and testament, it is a legal document that dictates what happens to your estate once you pass away. It makes it easier for the people you leave behind, as it designates beneficiaries and also an executor who will carry out your legal and financial wishes regarding your estate.

Please be sure to update your will every few years or when a major change occurs, such as marriage or divorce, births of grandchildren, beneficiary choices, changes in assets, or new tax laws. The will should be executed in the state in which you live. It can be simple or detailed, and it is best to consult a lawyer, though it also is possible to find templates online. Some people do their will using online resources as a placeholder until they can develop one with a lawyer's assistance.

Living Will

A living will is an advance directive, an instruction about whether or not the person wants to be resuscitated and kept alive in extremis. If you do not have a living will, your family may be faced with having to decide whether to withdraw life support. Some advance directives are included in the durable power of attorney for healthcare, but be sure to have that if yours is not. The living will, or advance directive, should be reviewed from time to time because your desires may change as your life develops. You can make changes any time you want.

Communication and Managing Information

We all have to go, to die, at some time. Sharing your wishes with your family is really important. Transparency is crucial. Family members need to understand what an older family member wants during life, during health situations, and after death. They need to know where key documents we have described here plus financial information (paper and computer) reside and where to locate the keys to the safety deposit box (and at which bank it resides), filing cabinet, and safe. They need access to the online passwords. They also need to know about your final wishes, as mentioned.

> *Cathy and her fiancé had a conversation on a long flight about their final wishes. Both were in good health and looking forward to their marriage and long life together. Weeks later, he was diagnosed with terminal brain cancer. Near the end, Cathy asked him simply whether he still wanted what he had said on the airplane. "Yes," he said softly.*

Some of the subjects covered here are awkward and often lead to tensions. But it is worth working through the discomfort to find the relief of knowing that planning is done. Whether it is your own planning or for your parents, you can get it done and go about the business of living. It will be a relief.

Do work through all these issues early. It will make your life easier and will be immeasurably valued by your children and/or caregivers. You could start now by writing three things you will research or tend to in the next two months about planning ahead, such as living will, lists for your kids, or checking out long-term care insurance.

Where to Keep Information

Health Insurance Information

Keep it all in one place, along with notes about coverage. This is when a good, clear filing system is needed. These documents do not need to be in a safety deposit box.

Financial Information

All of this information, sometimes collectively called estate planning, should be in one place. We urge writing the account numbers and key information all on one form, along with its location. (If an item is separated, make a note of what it is and where it is, such as "House deed is in the safety deposit box at Smith Bank.") This comprehensive listing document can be in your filing cabinet—preferably a locked filing cabinet—and also in the safety deposit box. You can use a form on our Website or a form your financial advisor provides. The items to be listed typically are life insurance policies, deeds, trusts, bank accounts, IRAs, Social Security, pensions, annuities, brokerage accounts, business legal documents, and passwords to electronic files.

Your Health Team of Experts

We suggest you assemble a team of formal and informal advisors as your Health Team of Experts. These are the people who will assist you or be by your side on all health matters. Some are experts you hire; others are experts you encounter online, on TV, on DVDs, or in books. The list includes your doctors, nutritionist, therapist, trainer, online or television exercise gurus, lawyer, eldercare expert, financial advisor, clergy, massage therapist, acupuncturist, Medicare helpline, and probably more. And resources you find on Google or your favorite search engine! And this book and its Appendix. Make a list and keep it handy. Include your confidants and family members who will be involved in your life and carrying out your wishes.

Be empowered and in charge. You are the CEO of your health. The future of your health will depend on the energy you put out every day. It's about the power of lifestyle and choices.

 Exercise 8-1: Being Proactive About Your Health

☐ Write down five ways that you will be proactive about your health in terms of exercise and eating habits. Be specific and set an early start date!

CHAPTER 9

Leaving Your Legacy

Carve your name on hearts, not tombstones. A legacy is etched into the minds of others and the stories they share about you.

—Shannon L. Alder

We all want to leave some sort of a legacy. It is human nature. One of the most natural ways to do that is through our children. We create, mold, and shape them. We instill them with our family values and stories. We look forward to seeing our children's children, our nieces and nephews, and our cousins' children, and we think of the continuation of our family name and genetics. We think about how to best articulate our values to our children so that they will continue our legacy. But there are many other ways we can leave a legacy, and Baby Boomers are as interested in this concept as they are in raising their children and grandchildren.

So what is a legacy? It is a way to make a difference. Leaving behind a part of yourself. A way to have others remember you. Building something that continues on. Making a difference in someone else's life. Influencing society. It is how you live your life and the people you touch. It can be ephemeral or physical. It can be financial or legal, in actions, or values. It is many things and the first questions you want to ask yourself are *What does it mean to me? What impacted me the most when I was growing up? What do I want to accomplish on this earth? What do I want to leave behind for others?*

This chapter is about leaving your legacy, in the best ways you are able to do it—for your family, your community, or the world. The following questions will help you to think about your own legacy as you read this chapter:

* Do you want to leave a legacy for your children? Your community? The world?

* What do you want that legacy to say about you? You are a leader? You are a great parent? You are kind? You are strategic? You are successful? You did so much for others or the community?

* Are you living your life so that it is a legacy to others?

* What are the most important messages you want your legacy to convey to others? Protect nature? Help those in need? Save money? Enjoy your family? Balance your life?

* Do you have the financial capacity to leave a large legacy, such as giving a major gift to a university? Building a building? Starting a foundation or nonprofit? Something else?

* What are some of the small ways you can leave a legacy or "make a difference"?

Types of Legacies

There are many kinds of legacies, including financial ones. We wanted first to show you ways that you can leave a legacy even if you are of modest means, so the financial discussion is at the end.

A Values Legacy

One of the most important legacies we all leave to our children and family is our values, whether we know it or not. It is exhibited often in the way we live our life. In fact, most of our values are implicit rather than explicit: how we treat people. How we feel about family. Our religious or spiritual beliefs. How we view money. How we work. How we view the world. How we value our friends. How we have integrity.

How are we articulating those values to our kids and grandkids? Certainly we demonstrate them every day in our actions, the stories we tell, what we say, and how we teach. Some families also are beginning to create a "values legacy" document. It is often used at family gatherings or included in their wills. It is a statement of the family's values and morals, and it is read to each generation at family events, such as births, deaths, and weddings, or at the time of the reading of the will. An exercise at the end of this chapter will help you in writing your own.

Giving Back

There are many ways you can give back to the community or world at large through involvement in your places of worship, nonprofits, hospitals and clinics, and educational institutions. You can volunteer your time. You can give and raise money for causes. You can serve on boards and provide leadership. You can help people one on one. Going back to the theme of how we articulate our values to our children, one of the best ways is for them to see how involved you are in the community and to be role models for them. This can be done by activities such as volunteering, or in a more dramatic fashion.

Cathy's father felt his legacy was in serving people. On his tombstone are the words, "We are put on this earth to serve our fellow men." He lived his life that way and hoped to instill the same values in Cathy and her brother. Cathy's father, by the way, was a banker, not a profession today always associated with serving others. But he used his platform of banking to help the community by bringing soybeans and crop rotation into the local area to enhance crop yield for the farmers, by building the first nursing home in Missouri to give assistance to the aging, by supporting the adoption of Medicare in the state to protect the vulnerable, and by having a dam and recreational lake built to enhance economic development in the region. He had a successful career, but he left a legacy of good works by using his knowledge, contacts, and position.

We all can ask ourselves if there is a way to leverage our company or position in it, in positive ways for the community. The trend toward companies looking at sustainability as part of their culture is but one example.

Connie was one of the first women managing directors for Goldman Sachs and had a very successful career. Goldman has a program to help women entrepreneurs. She left the position to start a nonprofit that provides livelihoods for women in Afghanistan who have lost their husbands or fathers or brothers and, by tradition in their villages, cannot leave the house. She created a company to market beautiful woven rugs from these women in the United States and elsewhere under the name of ARZU. In the process, she negotiated with the tribal elders—all men—that the proceeds of the sales would be shared with the village as well as the women, as long as it went to schools that allowed girls to attend. She not only helped with the economic livelihoods of the women and the village; she changed the attitudes toward education for girls. One person can make a difference!

When Marc Freedman began Encore, he knew that people who have had successful careers also had the drive to give back. His organization, discussed earlier in the book, helps people find ways to leverage their skills and talents into the nonprofit world and recognizes those who have really made a difference.

In the Appendix, we list a number of organizations in which you might want to get involved.

Creating a Family Foundation

With the help of your attorney and financial advisor, it is fairly simple today to create a family foundation, if you have the means and a vision. Many financial organizations, such as Synovus Financial's Family Advisory Management Service, offer services free as part of their overall financial relationship. For example, they have "boot camps" to help the younger generation understand about philanthropy, investing, and maintaining family wealth. They also provide services to help the family mediate issues where businesses or investments are involved. They help families decide succession planning and create ways to transfer wealth. There are tax benefits as well as legacy benefits to creating a foundation, and it is a way to involve family members early in leaving a family legacy. A foundation can be as inexpensive to start as $2,000 in legal and setup fees. Most people begin with at least $10,000 in funds.

> *Sally and Rob created a donor-directed family foundation within the local community foundation to support the arts in the Midwestern town where they both grew up. They had a strong interest in education and arts support and wanted to put their name and funding on something that supported the community and followed their passions. They both came from families that valued "giving back," and this was their way of individualizing it. Their daughter, an artist, and son, a philosophy major and executive in their family business, are both involved and see the foundation as something that will last much longer even than the family business. Together, family members decide how the funding will be allocated each year and how the new funds will be added to increase the endowment. It is a gift to their community, but also a gift to themselves by leaving behind a legacy.*

Often, foundations are created out of a tragedy to provide good for others.

> *The John Burke Foundation, part of the Washington Lawyers' Committee on Civil Rights, was created after John died of brain cancer at the relatively young age of 58. He had been general counsel to the Committee for more than 25 years and had helped start a nonprofit for public housing. The Foundation collected more than $100,000 in donations at his death, and it is still growing. Proceeds support efforts of the Committee in the areas of education and mentoring young school-age children, but also include helping to fund an annual breakfast honoring others who give back to the community. As important as the foundation is to the community, John's children get to understand all that their father did for others and how involved he was in things outside of work. It is a legacy that continues to teach them, as well as John's grandchildren.*

Creating a foundation focused on an issue or a cause or a passion is a great way to give back. There is much information on the web in terms of setting up foundations or ones that are already in existence. Try the Foundation Source Website (*www.foundationsource.com*) to get ideas.

Also look into crowdsourcing as a way to fund a foundation. It is being used for nonprofit as well as for-profit ventures. The Appendix has more information on this.

Many parents want their children to learn early about saving and giving, and a family foundation is one of the vehicles. It teaches them the right values and to be compassionate about others. It also teaches them about money management. One way some parents do this is by requiring one-third of every dollar the child receives as gifts or earnings go to philanthropy, one-third to savings, and one-third to their own wishes. Or the children are given an amount of money to "give back," and the parents work with them to learn about different nonprofits and their causes and allow the child to choose. And, of course, when old enough, the children become part of the family foundation board. Whatever works is good because it gets the kids involved early in both volunteering and giving money to issues they support.

Being a Public Servant

Though we might not be enthralled with our politicians in Congress right now, we all know amazing people in civic and government positions— local to federal—who have served our communities well. Whether it was serving on a school board or local county commission, or in a government agency, or as an appointed public policy person or a member of Congress or state elected official, there are many examples of legacies left through the public service by people we know. Their names may or may not be on public buildings or known only in local communities, but they made a difference. They served tirelessly, often for very little money, and tried to do the right thing by their constituents.

We all might want to think about how we can become more engaged in public policy. It might be running for office. It might be advising behind the scenes or fundraising. It might be as an activist for issues or a cause. Think about your passions and what is needed in your community as well as the world. You can write op-ed pieces and contribute. Think about the skills, knowledge, and contacts you have and how you can leave a legacy through giving back in this way. The civil rights movement was started by many small activist movements in local environments—people who had the courage to sit in the front of the bus or at a food counter that served only white people.

Constructing or Naming a Building, Wing, Bench, or Brick!

Like the business tycoons of the 19th and 20th centuries, there are many families who want to build something physical or, at least, name a building. Whereas many structures today are named for corporations or products, there are still many office buildings, recreational areas, school wings or rooms, community centers, and institutions that have naming opportunities for the right financial gift. If you are financially able to do this, check with your alma mater or local colleges, universities, sports facilities, hospitals, and housing developments for opportunities. A university campaign might have many naming rights for donation levels between $50,000 and $5 million for buildings, labs, or classrooms. You can also endow a chair position in your name within a college or department of the university, starting at $100,000.

Many museums across the United States have naming rights for wings or galleries. Be creative about your giving and look for ways to leave a legacy in an institution you are passionate about.

If you are of more modest means, as most of us are, there are still many opportunities. For example, for about $1,000 you can have an iron bench with your name put in a botanical garden or park. For about $500 you can plant a tree with your name on it. For $25 you can have your name on a brick in the walkway.

> *Often public buildings and recreational areas, parks, and bridges will be named after citizens and politicians who assisted in planning and developing the area or helped to secure funding. Cathy's father, mentioned before, worked tirelessly to get the Clarence Cannon Dam (named after the former congressman and chair of the House Appropriations Committee) and Mark Twain Lake built in northern Missouri. He and several other men had formed a committee to get Congress to appropriate the money for the Army Corps of Engineers to turn a yearly disaster of flooded farmland into a boon for the economy. For that dedication and work, Cathy's father has a large recreational area named for him, and the story of his legacy is in the museum connected with the dam. He had no money to "name" something, but his volunteer work created the same opportunity for a legacy.*

The Boomers, as a group, are active in philanthropy and want to make the world a better place. They do this in many ways, and creating their own nonprofits is one of them.

Cindy has a passion for history and science and spent much of her career working for the Federal government, including the U.S. Department of Energy (DOE). She was fascinated by the history of the Manhattan Project, the role of the national laboratories, and the leadership of J. Robert Oppenheimer. When she learned that DOE was planning to tear down most of the Manhattan Project properties at Los Alamos, she convinced the Advisory Council on Historic Preservation to intervene. After saving the most important properties, she persuaded DOE to apply for a Save America's Treasures grant. When the grant was awarded, she created the Atomic Heritage Foundation to raise money needed to match the grant. Now the properties where many of the early experiments took place and Oppenheimer's home in Los Alamos, New Mexico, will be preserved. These will be highlights of a new Manhattan Project National Historical Park that Cindy was instrumental in creating. The new park and the historic properties are a gift, not only to the community, but to the world at large.

Check with your community foundations, churches, schools, historical societies, and other nonprofit organizations for ideas that might fit with your passions.

Work Legacy

We spend a great deal of our waking hours at work. It is natural that it becomes a way that many people hope to leave a legacy. It might be by creating a new product or service, or a new division, or through a publication, invention, or patent. It might be by the new processes we create or the way we combine business and philanthropy. It might be through a legal case that changes the world.

Ginger was one of the few women to graduate from the Georgetown School of Law in the 1970s. She had always had an interest in the law. The Seventies were a time of much change, creating opportunities to challenge the status quo. Ginger was doing pro-bono work as part of her law firm's policies, and led, along with others, the effort to change the military academies' policies on allowing women to enter and graduate. What a legacy! Ginger directly impacted the ability of women to become officers in the military with the same prestigious education and status as men. That is a legacy that led to allowing women into more military fields, including flying and eventually combat, with more opportunity to advance to senior levels. Again, several people working together can make a difference!

There are many examples of how people have made a difference and left a legacy through work. They may have been an excellent boss. They may have been a terrific connector of people. They may have been the best marketer. Or visionary. What about you? What have you done to make a real difference in people's lives through your work? It can be as simple as being known for always acknowledging others' work so they feel appreciated, or the way you engage them in conversation.

Mentoring Legacy

Mentoring is another way to make a difference through others. Mentoring means taking an active interest in another and giving that person the advantage of your wisdom, knowledge, experience, and contacts. We do it every day without even thinking about it. Our teachers, clergy, friends, relatives, neighbors, doctors, lawyers, and bosses all have mentored us. And we mentor others. Think about your favorite teachers in grade or high school, and you can find a mentor that probably impacted your life—and you remember them, tell their story, and appreciate what they did for you. Who have been your important mentors? Have you had a chance to mentor another person the same way? There are a number of nonprofit organizations, such as Big Brothers and Big Sisters, that count on people wanting to mentor.

Supreme Court Justice Sonia Sotomayor is known as much for her mentoring of others as for her own stellar career. She was born of Puerto Rican descent in the projects in New York City. Her mother was one of her most important mentors. Justice Sotomayor was helped by many all along her career and made it her passion to mentor others, especially kids of Latino descent from the projects. She has been active in Latino/Hispanic organizations, schools, and nonprofits dealing with education. She wrote her autobiography to give hope and inspiration to others who are growing up in challenging circumstances. Justice Sotomayor is a mentor to many and will be remembered for that as well as being the first woman of Latino descent on the Supreme Court!

Building a Business

A large number of Boomers have created successful businesses and are now ready to hand them over to the next generation. This can be a gift or an albatross to our children. It can be a legacy, but a business can also be sold, fail, or be renamed. Think about how a business can be made sustainable, with or without your children running it, and how its mission can stay relevant and grow. Unfortunately, many Boomers' children do not want to take over their parents' businesses. They have different dreams or want to live in a different part of the country.

Have you thought about succession planning and how you can leave your legacy if your children are not involved? Many of your friends and relatives may depend on your business continuing. How do you accommodate them?

Creative Legacy

There are many ways you can leave a creative legacy for your children or the community. If you are a collector of art or items of artistic or historic import, you can pass that on to a museum or academic institution. If you are an artist yourself, you can pass on the actual art. And if you are neither, you can pass on your love of going to museums or the opera or ballet by taking your grandchildren, nieces, and nephews along with you. Not only will they have stories to tell about their adventures with you, they will likely develop the love of art and pass that down to their kids. Appreciation for art, music, dance, antiques, reading, writing, and other creative endeavors is a gift that you can instill in others. Think of tickets to an event rather than sweaters for the holidays for your family and friends!

John's grandmother always took her grandchildren on special trips throughout the year, but took the whole family each Christmas to a foreign country. These were not luxury trips in the best hotels. They were family trips, coach class and in rented apartments or houses where they could cook and have space to spend time with each other. They toured the countries and cities, went to museums, took in plays, and walked the streets to see the architecture. John grew up appreciating the value of travel, and learning the importance of observing others' customs and the value of experiences over things. He does the same thing for his grandchildren today.

Other ways to leave a creative legacy are by writing books, memoirs, plays, or music or producing movies. Or even being in movies, if you can!

Teresa's father was a jazz musician and a character and voice actor. He did voices for Disney, including the Indian Chief in Peter Pan. *He was also featured in several movies, including a memorable performance dancing with Fred Astaire. Teresa has copies of those movies and played them, first for her own son, and now for her grandchildren. She is able to see her dad perform and tell his story to each generation, and they will be able to do the same.*

Oh, the wonders of new technologies! You may not have the talent to be in a movie, but you can capture your singing or dancing or saxophone playing on a video and put it on YouTube to share with this generation, as well as the next. Think of ways you can share your creative passions with your family and encourage them to join you!

Many of us have creative capabilities. Some are artists professionally. Others of us dabble in everything from painting to photography to quilt-making to woodworking. Leaving a legacy of art or handcraft means that you have made things with your own hands and with your own creative expression for others to enjoy. It can be large and for the community or small and for a granddaughter. Either way, you are leaving a part of yourself to others.

Cathy still has the wooden rolling pin her grandfather made her grandmother when they got engaged. Rita still has the needlepoint cushions her mother and grandmother made. Nancy has quilts and crocheted items her Minnesota grandmother made. And Jaye celebrated her mother's good eye for photography when Christie's auctioned photographs by famous photographers from the 1940s through the 1970s that her mother had saved.

It is the stories that go with these items of art or craft that make them the legacy. Every time we use or look at one of the gifts handed down to us, it reminds us of who made or collected it. What better legacy? What do you have that you have made or collected, and have you told your stories about those items to your family?

>*Frank and his wife live in one of the old Charleston houses in the historic district. Over the years they have collected fine antiques, paintings, and old maps of Charleston, to fill the house. He has written a story about each of the maps, paintings, and furniture, and fixed it to the item, saying where he collected it, its value, and meaning. This way his children and grandchildren will have a better idea of what to keep, or give to a museum, or sell when he is no longer around. It gave him great joy to capture the "stories" of his collection, and his children are very appreciative.*

Telling Your Story

One of the easiest and most common ways to leave a legacy is to find a way to tell your story. Storytelling and oral history are arts often lost when we no longer have time to eat together at dinner or spend time on the front porch on a summer evening. We need to find ways to continue that tradition, maybe at holiday meals or by creating a special storytelling night each week with family members. Or plan reunions and include time for storytelling. Bring your video cameras, smartphones, and recorders to capture the moment and the stories.

>*Mel and his wife, Patricia, are both university professors. They have lived away from their Southern homes. But, to be sure their kids understand their family values and their "roots," they organize a yearly reunion in their hometown near Norfolk, Virginia. They have "story time" after the picnic dinner where the older members of the family talk about old times. It is the highlight of the reunion and, though some of the stories may be told over and over, that's okay. Stories are meant to be repeated and embellished!*

Other ideas that capture your stories are to write a memoir, write your obituary for the future, video family gatherings, interview and record family members, and take photographs.

Journaling and Scrapbooking

Angie has been journaling since 2005. She has more than 70 journals filled with her thoughts, ideas, and experiences for a significant period of her life.

It doesn't take much time or money to journal: just the cost of a notebook and a few minutes each morning. Writing in a journal is like a listening post to hear the whispers of your intuition. You begin to see patterns and to observe what might be going over the same issues in your life. You will likely want to keep some of the things you write in the journals private, but they can also give you much to share with others when, and how, you want to do that.

Ellen has been journaling since she was a young girl. Her journals include thoughts, sketches, morning pages, itineraries, and many other things that help her remember a trip, a special occasion, or a summer vacation with her grandchildren. She shares her journals with her family and friends and plans to give them to her oldest granddaughter. She has her thoughts in the journals, but edited them as she wrote, knowing they would be shared in the future.

Scrapbooking is another way to preserve family history and leave a legacy. All you have to do is go to a Michael's or an A.C. Moore store near you to see how important scrapbooking is to the public. You can find any type of book, paper, accessories, or help in capturing your family's photos, papers, events, and memories. The scrapbooks might have a theme, such as an engagement and wedding, or the birth of a child. Or it might be about someone's professional career. One of our former Retreat attendees has a scrapbooking business and Website at *www.apagefromyourlife.com*.

Writing a Memoir

Memoirs are becoming more popular, either for public consumption or for private family use. Think of Frank McCourt's *Angela's Ashes* and you think of the impact these books have had. A memoir, unlike biographies or autobiographies, which are based in research and fact, is a collection of stories from our memories, often about a special time in our lives. It must be truthful, but the facts are blurry, as are our memories, and we write from feeling rather than research.

To write a memoir, you need to set the context and decide whether you are writing it for your family and friends or whether there is a more appealing and universal theme to the concept that would make it interesting for public consumption. Themes such as redemption, coming of age, survival, and self-reflection are popular reads and might be of interest to a publisher or e-reader. You will need to think about privacy and how much you want to share or not, but a memoir is a wonderful way to capture your legacy. There are a number of books and courses on writing memoirs. The Cape Cod Writers Center Conference in August each year has a number of good teachers and courses. Most local colleges and universities or writers groups do as well. Today's self-publishing options allow you to publish your own memoir for your family or for the larger community.

Paul's great-great grandfather was a Methodist Circuit Rider in southern Colorado in the 1880s and later a founder of Southern Methodist University in Dallas, Texas. Paul is writing a memoir that combines the writings of his great-great grandfather with his own life observations. Although they lived several generations apart, he remembers his great-great grandfather from when he was a boy and the stories he would tell about riding his horse through the desert in New Mexico to go to a Methodist convention in Albuquerque, or how he tried, unsuccessfully, to convert cowboys to stop drinking. Although he is writing only for his family, Paul will put the writings about his great-grandfather in the context of the time, when the West was wild, the Gold Rush was on, and western towns began to become civilized.

Video or Photographs

The growth of video production at an amateur level due to smartphones, tablets, and YouTube has created the means to capture family activities, sayings, occasions, and missteps instantly and share them at will. A far cry from needing special film and cameras, your smartphone can do almost as good a job, and you can transmit the images in many ways to others as well as store it for the future. In fact, one of the documentaries that won an Oscar recently based on the life of a blues musician was shot all on an iPhone. There are apps on phones that allow you to edit what you have shot, enhance it, make it look like a vintage film, or add music in the background. You become your own writer, director, actor, and producer. A perfect way to capture voice and age over time!

Many colleges and universities and photography schools are teaching the art of filmmaking by iPhone or iPad. Go online to find the apps and join a class to perfect your skills. Both Microsoft and Apple have classes, as does YouTube.

The advent of digital photos has changed everything, from the device you use (more photos are taken in the world today with smartphones than cameras) to the way you share them, through Websites. It is now easy to create yearly photo albums or special occasion albums, where you can have cropped pictures, comments, and additional documentation. One idea is to create a grandparents book for your grandchildren that includes photos from various generations and their stories, maybe a family tree, and your story in more detail. Include your "values chart" as well. There are courses online and at area schools and photography shops that can get you started. Start organizing those images now! Software and apps exist to help you, such as Snapfish, Shutterfly, Picasa, Instagram, and Pinterest. Desktop publishing is affordable and available to everyone.

Leaving a Fortune, Large or Small

And last, but not least, the more common way people have created a legacy is to leave financial trusts and gifts to be handed down generation to generation. There are many ways to do this, from creating 529 College Accounts for your grandchildren, to leaving up to $14,000 per year to any family member tax-free, to leaving a trust with stipulations. A trust can help start a child in life or fund an education or launch a business. According to a recent survey by Wealth Counsel, more than 35 percent of people are crafting their estate plans to avoid mismanagement by their heirs. They suggest talking to your heirs to lay out your desires for your legacy. You can give them an option of taking a financial course or talking to a financial planner, or give them practice in managing their money through the gifts you give each year. They might make mistakes, but they will learn before they receive the larger amount.

An alternative is to set up a trust with a trustee to have oversight on the inheritance to be sure it is used as you intend. These usually cost about $1,600 to $3,000 to set up by an estate attorney, and require a friend, family member, or bank that you appoint, to administer the trust. You can also attach some strings, such as forcing heirs to complete college or stagger the trust or require drug tests before receiving the inheritance.

This idea of leaving a great deal of money to your heirs is beginning to fall out of favor, however—first by the tech executives, and also by Warren Buffett, who believes his money should impact society now rather than leave it to his kids. Many financial advisors also counsel that leaving money to your children often is a curse as well as a blessing. Many of the kids begin to think they are "entitled" to the fortune and do not need to earn their own living or even continue their education. They are sometimes referred to as "trustfunders," and many have not had happy lives. In fact, the phrase *shirtsleeve to shirtsleeve in three generations* refers to this lack of motivation of the children of the wealthy, where they know a large amount of money is coming their way. At any rate, think about the impact on values and what legacy you really want to leave. Money is not always the answer.

Whatever you decide to do about leaving money to your family, it is critically important that you have a will and see a lawyer or estate planner to be sure you direct and control what happens, and that, in fact, what you wanted to have happen, does. Writing a will without benefit of legal and financial advisors or not having a will at all, usually ends in disaster.

The Most Important Way to Leave a Legacy: How You Live Your Life

We are mentors and role models to others, from our children to the community and the world. We have the ability to influence by our actions, as well by as our words and deeds—by the way we treat people, by how authentic we are, by the value we put on integrity and character, and the way we show our compassion and humanity. It is all in the choices we make. Here are some examples; add your own to this list:

* Knowing that we can make a difference.
* Taking responsibilities for our choices.
* Giving thanks for every blessing.
* Listening with our hearts.
* Committing random acts of kindness.

Having the Conversation With Your Kids

We have talked throughout this chapter about the importance of being role models for our children and leaving a legacy that way. But how do we begin the discussion? Pick a time that is relaxed or poignant. It might be a vacation; it might be a family dinner; it might be after a memorial service. The point is to use times in your life to share your values, such as creating or reading from the "values statement" or telling stories that have a point. Use every opportunity to bring in a story from the past that relates to a current event, especially if there is a moral to the tale!

Your actions speak, too.

Rita launched her photographic accomplishments in a gallery in December 2013. It was the first time her work had been shown publicly. She had never done a thing in photography until two years before, and took courses and just shot and shot. She did not think of herself as a creative person. But she loved it and has created some amazing and beautiful images. The show was both scary and fulfilling for her, as she had worried whether people would come and what if they didn't buy? But the real point of the show was to teach her two sons that you can do anything if you try and are willing to get out of your comfort zone. She is giving them the legacy of taking risks and being creative. What a wonderful gift for them.

Projects you might want to do with your kids beyond the "values statement" are to create a family memoir, do a scrapbook or photo book of family history, research your genealogy, video family stories, or create a family foundation, to start. And bring out those photos or old yearbooks or antiques, and start telling their stories!

Ancestry and DNA Research

The proliferation of sites like Ancestry.com and the introduction of DNA tests, such as those from National Geographic and 23andMe, are examples of new services and products to fulfill this need of Boomers to leave a legacy. There are services to help you develop your genealogical tree as far back as the 1400s and DNA tests to see if your forefathers came from Asia Minor or Europe. There are tests to see if you have a genetic propensity to diabetes or should avoid certain drugs or foods.

The Church of Jesus Christ of the Latter-Day Saints (Mormon) has long researched genealogy and offers data as well as services to those searching for their roots. Countries like Ireland, from which many people migrated to the United States, have services to help Americans find their original family counties, towns, and relatives. Ireland's "The Gathering" 2013 summer promotions were targeted to Americans with Irish ancestry. This "ancestry travel" will only get bigger as DNA tests provide more accurate information about one's heritage. Boomers will be big buyers as they retire and have more time and inclination to search. Does your family have a family tree? Old Bibles with records of births and deaths? Aunts who have researched your family heritage? If not, get busy and start researching. Ancestry.com is one place to start.

What will you choose to do to leave a legacy? Talk this over with your spouse or partner as well as children. A legacy implies that others will go along, accept, or "buy in" to the values and ideas you put forward. What better project for the family! That in itself is a legacy!

✎ Exercise 9-1: Creating a Family Values Statement

Create a values statement for your family, based on the comments earlier in the chapter, and use it as a way to start telling stories to your family. Ask your elder relatives to participate and find a way to capture their stories through videos and recordings.

❐ With the values you hold dear written down, explain why each one is important to you and who or what influenced you to care about that value.

❐ Pick 10 of the values you think are the most important and write them in a way they can be duplicated and framed for your family. Give them as gifts and encourage your family to put them where they will see them every day.

CHAPTER 10

Simplifying Your Life and Living a Life of Passion

The wisdom of life consists in the elimination of nonessentials.

—Lin Yutang

Many Boomers are reaching the stage of de-acquisition, that period of time where we want to stop acquiring things, and start giving them away or selling them. It might be to downsize a house or as part of a move. It might be because our children need things to start their households. But it is often because we want to simplify our lives—what we own and how we live. This final chapter is meant to help you focus on ways to simplify your life so that you may have more time to follow your passions and live the way you want.

Our friends, at first, laughed at the idea of the four of us writing a chapter about simplifying our lives. They said, "But your lives are already so busy, and now you are adding writing a book!" In fact, "simplifying your life" means different things to different people. Some people are high energy and involved in many things, but it is what they love to do, and it is not stressful to them. Others use "busyness" at times to avoid things that scare them, or people or tasks they want to avoid. Still others can't wait for the time to have unscheduled days when they can do what they want, when they want, even if it is reading a book cover to cover, or spending a day hiking in the woods, or sitting on the beach listening to the gulls and breaking waves.

This is a new life chapter for you, and you want to make sure you are prioritizing those things that make your heart sing—those passions you now have more time to follow. Think about what simplicity means to you before you begin this chapter and see how your definition might change by the end.

Simplicity is the art of making choices, treasuring precious moments, and valuing that which is of worth to us, whether spiritual, intellectual, or physical. It is finding abundance in small things. It is focusing attention on what we want to create and experience. It is finding a balance between "being" and "doing." The bedrock of simplicity is integrity, the true integration of who we are and how we live. It is being authentic.

In this chapter we talk about ways you can simplify your life, career, finances, home, belongings, relationships, vacations, and daily chores in order that you have more time to follow your passions. Simplifying is part of the process of transitioning to the new lifestyle you are planning.

The Gift of Time: Quieting Your Mind

To simplify your life, you first need to still your mind. And that is hard to do when you have deadlines, work, family, interruptions, activities, and obligations. To really be ready to find simplicity in your life, you need to give yourself the "gift of time" we talk about in our book *Reboot Your Life*. In it we discuss the importance of taking time off from work, family obligations, or other things that distract us, to be able to give ourselves quiet time to plan what we want to do next and to understand and follow our passions.

This well-known adage is so true: "You must nourish yourself to be able to nourish others." It means we need to take time for ourselves in order to be rested and open to being there for others. So it is not a selfish act to take time. We are just preparing ourselves to be there for our family, friends, and colleagues, in this next chapter of life.

There are many ways to achieve simplicity in our minds. Yoga and other meditative exercise, walking in nature or a park, doing tai chi, journaling, meditating, praying, listening to classical music, and sitting on a beach are just some of the ways we clear the chaos in our minds.

We can do it best when we detach from technology. Silence our smartphones. Stay away from e-mail, Instagram, Twitter, LinkedIn, and Facebook. Turn off the TV. The point is, clear out the clutter in your mind to be able to clear out the clutter in your life.

Simplifying Your Daily Life

Some of the most common laments we get when we have had retreats or interviewed people about this next chapter is "Our lives are so complex" or "We are too busy" or "I just need someone to organize my life." We all feel overwhelmed with the many responsibilities we have, so this chapter is an attempt to give you some of the hints and "best practices" we have found from others about how to clear some of that chaos and leave more time to enjoy the things we really want to do.

Appointment Calendars, Schedules, and Lists

Just because you have retired from your job, it doesn't mean that you have to give up administrative support. Even if you never had your own, you may need it now. This section addresses some of those issues.

Although many of us keep our calendars on our computers or smartphones, we have found there are a few other, simpler ways to help keep track of what we have on our plates. One is to keep a paper calendar as a backup to the electronic, but more importantly because it allows you to see a day, a week, or even a month at a glance. This is helpful in looking ahead at how much you have to do and to schedule in downtime or weekends away, or just seeing when you have loaded too much into a time period. Buy an attractive day timer cover and use paper inserts for Day at a Glance. For the next year's planning, buy a calendar that is a month at a time and start filling in known dates before you get your Day at a Glance refills. This may sound retro, but many people feel it is the best way. Many families use a blackboard or huge calendar on the kitchen wall to plot out all their activities as a reminder of what they have to do each week.

> *Joann and Bob use individual electronic calendars, but have a master annual paper calendar with both schedules that they both can see. They update the joint calendar frequently, and it helps them to negotiate and live peacefully together.*

And then there are the lists—on sticky notes, on the back of an envelope, on a scrap of paper, in the notebook, and everywhere else we found a place to write. Or in our smartphones, or laptops, but not all in one place. Some people use an electronic or paper "List Book" where they capture all their "to dos" into one place, segmented by topic, such as House or Work or whatever they need to think about. Having them all in one book or electronic record allows you to keep adding to the lists by category and cross them off when done.

Cathy uses a spiral-bound notebook with graph paper in colored sections inside. She carries it everywhere, adds things she needs to do, and loves the pleasure of crossing off those she has finished. She has lists by section of things she needs to do for Business, Boards, Non-profits, Grandkids, House, Holidays, Finances, Health, Friends and Family, and Writing and Consulting for Reboot Partners. The only thing that doesn't go into the book is her grocery list. In the front section, she writes daily things that need to be done. It is a way to help make her complex life simple.

Asking for Help

Behind every organized person, there is a team that helps! It may be our spouses or partners, kids, siblings, employees, neighbors, friends, or people we pay, such as housekeepers, gardeners, assistants, delivery personnel, or babysitters. Having an "advisory board" of people to help us sort through things like finances or healthcare, is so important. But some of us need help in our everyday life as well. Think about who might be on your Team of Experts.

We gripe about our kids or grandkids not being very helpful or responsible for chores such as cleaning their rooms or doing the tasks we assign them. Maybe we are going about it the wrong way. Having a family problem-solving meeting might reframe the issue. And making the effort joint and fun!

Alison would set a timer and have her daughter and son work with her to clean out a closet or the kitchen drawers together in a specific time period. They would decide what they would tackle, how they would do it, and for how long. They would reward themselves at the end with some treat, but it was the laughter and doing it together that made it fun and accomplished what needed to be done.

Personal Assistants

You might say, "Oh, I could never afford a personal assistant" or think, "That is too unnecessary or pretentious." Try another way of looking at it: Your time is your most valuable asset, and for every errand that takes you three hours to do, you could be taking your granddaughter to the local museum. There are many people out there who need part-time jobs, and you would be helping them, as well as yourself. Maybe it is a mom with small children or a recent retiree, someone new to the country, or a college student. Think about the things that having a person one day a week or three afternoons might be able to do to help you. Think of it as another way to give back—to them as well as yourself. Some good places to look are:

* Colleges and universities.
* Online administrative services.
* Temporary agencies.
* Monster.com.
* Through friends or your church or synagogue.

Grace shares an assistant with another friend. Together, they use the assistant four days a week, but because they know each other, they can alter the schedule when needed. It works for everyone, and the assistant is like another part of the family. She does everything from shopping, to scheduling, to wrapping gifts, to entering data on the computer, to helping plan parties. What a gift to all!

Keep the Housekeepers

Some people like to take care of their houses and have the time to do so, but most of us end up having to do the cleaning and sorting on weekends, vacations, or at night. And that keeps us from having our own personal time or time with family and friends. So what are some ways to help? If you have a housekeeper, keep her, even if you are retired or taking a career break. Do not feel guilty. You are giving someone else a job who needs it, and it is another way of giving back. If you cannot afford someone every week, try every other week. Or share a housekeeper with someone else. If you cannot afford that, ask a friend to help you one day with your house cleaning and you help that friend another day. Doing it together takes less time and is more fun. But the point is to find ways to delegate the daily living tasks to others or share them so that you simplify your life and free up more time for yourself.

The Value of Camps and Babysitters

Paul had this vision that his grandchildren and their mother could visit for the summer. He thought it would be wonderful for them to enjoy his house, his pool, and Cape Cod. He thought they could be entertained with time at the beach, books, swimming, videos, and miniature golf, and that he would be able to go to work and come home to play and read to them. But in his vision he did not take into account the fact that their mother did not drive or swim, and that the kids were only 3 and 5. Watching videos for them was a five-minute—at best—activity! The kids were bored while he was at work and wanted him to play and take them places when he got home. After the first week, he was exhausted! Fortunately for everyone, he was able to get the kids into a day camp, which had age-appropriate activities, and they loved it! They could now play with other kids, swim at the camp's pool with lifeguards, learn new things, and have great memories. And their mother and Paul had some time to themselves, so that when the kids were at home each day after camp and on the weekends, they loved being together.

The importance of babysitters, nannies, camps, and other scheduled activities for kids and grandkids should be a component of your planning. Many grandparents we interviewed, though loving their kids and grandkids, felt overwhelmed when they visited or felt used by their kids as "babysitters." Putting boundaries around your time is critical to simplifying your life. Finding ways to accommodate grandkids and kids, but still have free time, should be your goal.

Detaching From Technology

As much as we enjoy and need our electronics, they can often control our lives and make them more complex. If we are constantly "on," we are distracted from doing other things that might bring us simple pleasures or the quiet we seek. There are even "detach" or "unplug" movements that promote leaving your smartphones, tablets, laptops, and other electronics off on weekends or at the end of the day or at dinner or kept out of the bedroom. Some go as far as banning TV and radio as well, one day a week. There are studies that show how addicted we are to our smartphones and social media. Many have focused on the harm to children by spending too much time on electronic media, especially before the age of 3.

Think about ways you and your family can detach from electronics, at least to start, during meal times. Or for one evening a week. Build up until it might be a weekend or even a vacation. There are so many wonderful things to do besides being online or sitting in front of a television. Take a walk in nature or at your local park. Go to a museum. Go fishing. Take a nap. Paint a picture. Play board games or cards. Enjoy the simple pleasures.

You might say, "But what will my friends think if I am not online?" or "I might miss something." Really, you won't. Just try it.

Simplifying Your Work

Of course, a big factor in how complicated our lives are is in what we do for a living. It is why many people want to retire. However, they soon learn they are as busy as when they were working. You may actually have to schedule in "downtime" or time to rest. Put it on your calendar and let people know certain days are sacrosanct to you.

Keeping Your Job Simple

If you think about your career, it may seem as if you have more than one job. If you can, think about ways you can have one job and one responsibility, rather than several. What does that mean? It could be choosing not to be in consulting or a career where you have many customers, not working in a law firm where you have to constantly find new clients, not having several projects due at the same time. Your job may not allow you this kind of simplicity, but if you can clear the decks at work a bit, you will have more time to do other things you love. A number of people we talked to who had very complex and stressful careers have chosen to work, in their retirement, in some retailing jobs or in some field that allows them to go home at night without thinking about the job. They have simplified their work to leave time for other things.

Limits on Corporate Boards and Consulting

If you are already on corporate or private company boards, or want to be on them, you probably already know that "best practice" is to be on no more than three boards. Today's boards are demanding, with committee work, governance oversight, and activist shareholders. The more boards you are on, the harder to juggle mandatory committee meetings and vacation time. Most corporations have limits on board participation, for good reason. Set as your goal no more than three, and if you are fully employed, maybe only one. Boards, corporate or nonprofit, however, are a wonderful way to continue to influence business, network, and continue learning. Don't be afraid to make changes along the way, gracefully amending board/volunteering commitments for a better fit or more free time. Sometimes you have to learn this by trial.

In the same way, many people continue in their fields after leaving their main employer by consulting. This, too, can be all-consuming, so put boundaries around the number of clients you want to have or the type of consulting you will do. Think of providing advisory services, which generally are one-day or retainer types of "on call" consulting. This is easier than trying to hire and manage others to help you with full-blown project consulting. As you design your next chapter, planning the voids or the downtime is as important as planning what you do.

Putting Boundaries on Volunteering

Many of us who have worked all our lives are so excited to have time to get more involved in nonprofits by volunteering or sitting on their boards or going to their events. This is just a reminder to pick the two to three nonprofits that best fit your passions. Pick where you can have the most impact or where you will have the most fun or where there is the most need. But only pick a few. If others ask for help, you can always write a small check, but guard your time so that you can give effectively and still have time for yourself.

Simplifying Your Home

Our homes are our refuges, our places to get away and relax, our safety nets, our places to entertain friends and spend time with family. But they also are our catch-alls, storage lockers, project keepers, and where we come home and eat and sleep amidst our busy lives. All too often, they become part of our stress—the disposal that stops working, the garage that no longer can accommodate the car because it has become the store-room, the closet doors that won't shut. How can we simplify our homes so that they become the refuges we need? We want them to provide us with serenity and a place to refresh and relax. How do we do that?

Removing the Clutter

Boomers have been known as the "consumption generation." We have fueled the economy, and filled our homes with things we love and maybe some we don't. We have inherited things from our parents and grandparents. We have loved going to yard sales and finding treasures. We have received one too many vases or bowls or candlesticks as gifts. We just plain have too much stuff. What to do? We get overwhelmed. We avoid the attic and basement and forget the garage!

But this can also be a time when parents give away the "treasured items" that adult children or grandchildren mourn later in life. Be sure to offer things clearly and first to adult children, siblings, or others who might inherit your belongings. Give the boxes of memories and scrapbooks to your children now, if they have the space and stable lifestyle to take them. Make an inventory of potentially valuable things you own, and if your children don't want them, liquidate and put it in your savings!

Though we love our things and want to hold the memories, there is a freedom in letting go, especially if someone else can enjoy them. Go to www.realsimple.com/organizedhome for some great ideas. Here are a few tips we learned from others, as well:

* **Break down sorting into chunks of time.** Do one room at a time, or one closet at a time.

* **Involve the family.** Get everyone to help sort his or her own space and to work as a team to tackle the big jobs.

* **Hire a professional.** There are people who will help you organize your closets, clothes, kitchen, garage, and/or other spaces. They work with you to sort piles into things to keep, give away, throw away, and sell. Sometimes they will actually sell things for you on eBay and take a commission.

* **Get a friend to help.** Trade off helping each other in each other's homes. Be the critic for her as she is for you.

* **Re-gift things where you see a need.** If you really don't need it or like it, there is always someone who does. Give things to your kids, siblings, friends, work associates.

* **Give things to charity.** The Salvation Army, Boys and Girls Clubs, Habitat for Humanity, Goodwill, churches, synagogues, and many other organizations will take donations of everything from your car to furniture to clothing to architectural items.

* **Have a great sale.** You can hold a yard sale, join a community one, sell things online through Craigslist and eBay, or take them to consignment stores. If you have valuable art, antiques, coins, designer clothing, or other things like that, it is worth it to look at consignment places and the online sales venues. If really valuable, have them appraised by a reputable appraiser.

This doesn't mean you don't still collect things you love! Just view it as curating or editing down your collections (whether they are shoes, antique quilts, sports equipment, or lamps) to what you really love and need, and opening up space for something new! Having your Team of Experts include friends or professionals to help with these tasks can be enormously beneficial.

The Hidden Value of Downsizing

Many Boomers are downsizing, often moving to smaller cities or from the suburbs back into urban centers, into apartments, condos, and lofts.

The downsizing may be driven by costs, tax advantages, desire for freedom, or the ability to walk to places. Realtors and developers are seeing this trend, and creating renovated and new housing in urban areas and in small towns, especially those with colleges and universities.

Moving to a smaller apartment or home from a larger one has many advantages beyond the obvious financial ones. It forces us to sort and prioritize the things we want to keep and those we can sell or give away. It forces us to keep things simpler and less cluttered. It forces us not to have much in storage. And it gives us more time to play because we have less need to clean, organize, or maintain. Better yet, it gives someone else the responsibility for maintenance. Just making the move to less space often makes our lives simpler. One often-incorrect premise is that your children and grandchildren will be spending a lot of time in your home. As the kids grow and are busy with their own lives, family gatherings may be at their homes or at a vacation destination, and you may end up dusting empty guest rooms for years to come!

> *Tom and Katy have launched their three kids into college and jobs. They now have their four-bedroom home on the market and can hardly wait to move. The process of getting the house ready to sell made them sort and give away or sell much of what they had. They worked with their kids to sort their clothes, sporting equipment, and other stuff and limited what they would continue to store for them. Katy and Tom are building a smaller home on the side of a hill that will also be planted with grape vines for Tom's dream of having a vineyard. It has room to grow a large garden for heirloom vegetables, another passion. The house will be much easier to maintain and clean and will be less expensive but serve their new life much better. Katy was as excited about getting rid of stuff as she was planning the new space. She said it was like "starting a new chapter" in their lives.*

Fewer Places and Less Ownership of Homes

Many Boomers have second homes or two locations because of work. It can be double the fun, but also double the trouble.

> *John and Susan decided to sell their condo in Washington, DC, as well as their second home in Florida to simplify their lives. Both*

homes required a good deal of attention and much of John's time. They now rent a house in Virginia to lessen the responsibilities and have more free time. They bought a condo for their future retirement in Florida for the same reason: Someone else has to worry about the roof leaking or the lawn care. They can enjoy both places, without the hassle.

It's not that we are saying don't have a second home, because, in fact, many of us have them. It's just getting us all to acknowledge the time it takes, as well as the money, and calculate that into our plans. Are there ways to simplify having a second home?

One way to have the pleasure of living in several places, but not the maintenance, is the trend we have talked about in other chapters of trading your home with friends, or through Websites such as VRBO, *www. homeexchange.com*, or *www.homeaway.com*.

Braden has done this a number of times with his home in Ireland. Most recently, he and his wife and family stayed in Cape Cod for a week at a home that he traded for his in Kenmare, Ireland. It is a wonderful way to experience living elsewhere, with all the comforts of a home without the hassle of maintenance.

Assigning Tasks in the Family

This is one of the most important "gifts" we can give ourselves and others: sharing the responsibilities in a home. Whether it is your spouse or partner, your kids or grandkids, or your parents or other relatives living with you, the concept of "sharing a home" means also sharing in taking care of it. Enlist help in sorting and getting rid of clutter, in taking care of one's own possessions, in cleaning up for company, in fixing things that are broken, and so on. You are not the only one responsible. Plus, it teaches good manners, how to be good guests in others' homes, how to take care of their own home one day, and how to be thoughtful of others.

Joan remarried and now has an extended family of five kids, their spouses and partners, and seven grandchildren. Her husband's kids had grown up not having to participate in taking care of the home or having tasks, such as helping with the dishes or getting ready for company. This caused problems early in Joan and Rick's relationship because she felt the kids viewed her as the "maid" and were not thoughtful. She did several things to change that. She expressed her feelings to the kids and asked them to help when they could. Her husband helps with all tasks, showing the kids that it is part of being in a family. They are beginning to get the message and now, at least, help with the cooking or understand the tradeoffs in having a home-cooked meal!

You See It, You Use It

How many of us have kitchen cabinets full of stuff we rarely use or closets full of clothes we never wear? Part of the issue is not seeing what we have and reverting to the closest thing. One of the new design features for kitchens is open shelving, in which you stack dishes and glassware where you see it and it becomes part of the décor. It certainly encourages you to sort through and give away those burned-out pots or chipped and un-matching bowls! The concept is to find ways to store things that you can see, so you will use them. The Container Store has wonderful assortments of clear bins for storage that can be labeled.

> *Jenny has a beautiful pantry—yes, beautiful. Everything is in clear, labeled containers and on clean white shelves. She can easily see and reach anything she needs to prepare meals. As our grandmothers used to say, "A place for everything and everything in its place."*

For your clothes, change out for the season so that there is more room, and each season look at what you did not wear and put it in a bag for Goodwill. Use clear containers for purses, sweaters, shoes, ties, belts, and other accessories. Hang necklaces on hooks on the wall. Sort clothes by type and color or put together in outfits that work. Find shoe racks to make more room on the floor.

One fun idea is to have a clothes-swapping party where everyone brings a set amount of clothes, accessories, and shoes, and trades them with others. Stuff left over goes to Goodwill. Make it a party and be sure to have plenty of mirrors!

Simplifying Your Finances

We spent quite a bit of time on finances in **Chapter 3: Making Your Money Last,** so we won't dwell on them here except to say this is an area that seems to get increasingly complex as we get older and one where we need to ask for help to make it as simple to understand and manage as possible.

Talk to the Experts

Make sure that you have people you trust, and several you talk to, when you are making financial decisions. Your Team of Experts should include professionals like CPAs, Certified Financial Planners (CFPs), and lawyers, as well as your banker, and your relatives or friends who have financial savvy. Even they will have differing opinions, but it will make sure you have as much knowledge as possible. Read magazines such as *Money* and *Consumer Reports on Money* and AARP publications for ideas. Attend seminars at your local church, community center, college, or university.

Get it Organized

Getting your information all in one place is critical. It might be in files or you might use a program like Quicken to have it online—whatever works for you. Have everything in a central place, such as your office or in a file box in your bedroom closet.

Keep it to Three Relationships

Pare your financial relationships and accounts to three organizations. Having more accounts or money at one institution usually gets you better rates and service, but still diversify your banks and investment firms. Inquire into what it takes to be eligible for personal banking rates.

Let Your Family Know

One of the biggest mistakes we often make is not letting our partners or spouses or children know about our finances. They need to know where we have accounts, where we keep our information, what our passwords are to the online information, where the keys to the safety deposit box might be, who our advisors are, where our wills are stored, and many other things that will help them, should we become ill or incapacitated. This is not just for older people; this is for everyone, because we never know what might happen. Having everything in a central place and in a notebook is critical.

Narrow Your Philanthropy Focus

One way to simplify your finances concerns how you give to nonprofits, your place of worship, and your alma mater. If you narrow your focus to follow your passions or interests in giving, and give more to each place, you will make a greater impact, and it will be appreciated. You can always give a small amount for a friend's charity event or your child's school event, but save your larger amounts for more directed giving. Let people know your objectives and say you only give to education or cancer research or to victims of poverty. You can change your goals each year, but try to give more to a smaller number of organizations.

Simplifying Your Vacations

We all love to take vacations and spend time with family and friends, but these can be as stressful and challenging as your regular life. How can they be simplified? How can they become the time when we can refresh and renew and enjoy ourselves? Following are some of the suggestions from people we talked to:

* **Be flexible about travel,** not only to get last-minute good deals, but also just to throw your bags in the car and take off, without a plan!

* **Go on preplanned trips** such as educational trips through your college or university where they have made all the arrangements.

* **Go on cruises,** especially on smaller ships, where there are fewer people and still many activities for people of all ages.

* **Trade or rent a house** in another country or town and explore just that area from the house each day.

* **Go with a group of friends** and each take a portion of the trip to organize, such as where you will stay, how you will be transported, what you will see, where you will eat, and where are the best places to shop.

* **Have the "one bag" rule** where you can only take enough clothes or accessories that fit into one bag—even better if it is a carry-on.

* **Rent equipment** such as bikes, snorkels, golf clubs, and tennis rackets when you need them rather than carrying them with you.

* **Use online resources** for where to go and what to do. Your smartphone apps have great information, and you can ditch the paper books.

* **Do a staycation** and stay at home, but promise not to do any chores. Go out to eat or order in. Visit all the area museums, plays, stores, and take hikes and bike rides. Enjoy your hometown as a visitor!

* **Visit friends** and let them plan what you do.

Simplifying Your Relationships

Simplifying your life also includes simplifying your relationships. In fact, it may be the drama and the drain of relationship obligations that are the biggest timewasters. Although it may sound hard-hearted to say some relationships have to go, think of it as freeing you to spend more focused time on the ones you cherish, including yourself.

Figure Out Your Inner Circle

Think of time as a limited resource, and create circles of family and friends who are important to you. There is the inner circle of family and friends with whom you want to spend time and who make you feel good. And then there are circles of people you like, but on a limited basis: acquaintances, work colleagues, church associates, nonprofit friends, and others. As an exercise, do at least four circles and put people, regardless of whether they are family, friends, or new to you, in circles going out from most interesting and fun to be around to least. Surprised by where people fall? A sibling might be in that outer circle because of his personality or political views. A friend from church, even though you don't know her that well, might be on the inner circle. The idea is that we choose our friends and our inner circle. They do not necessarily fit there just because they are family. Think about this is terms of managing relationships. Those family members who are important to you and friends you like for specific reasons might be in the circle where you meet them for a movie or dinner or invite once a year to a party. The ones in your inner circle might be the ones you travel with or see each week. Allocate your time by fun and passion, not obligation.

Jettison Relationships that Don't Work

Some members of the family or friends may be just too much of a drain or provide too much drama to continue a relationship. To be fair to yourself and them, try to first have a long talk with the friend or family member, or write a letter expressing your concerns and sadness that your relationship doesn't seem to be working. Maybe that person has had some difficult times you don't know about or you have done something, unintentionally, that offended him or her. Try to find a way to continue, maybe limiting the times together. But if that doesn't work, do not feel guilty about saying, "I just can't make this relationship work right now," and try to separate on terms as friendly as possible. Who knows? Maybe 10 years from now that person will be different, and you can reconnect. Freeing yourself from destructive or unproductive relationships frees you to spend more time with others who are positive and fun.

Have Smaller Events to Create More Intimacy

It is much easier, and more intimate, to have smaller gatherings and simpler events to allow time to focus on the people, not the food or environment. The simpler the better. Another couple for dinner. Three girlfriends going out to a movie. A road trip with your best friend. A Sunday evening bridge game. Keep it simple by having everyone bring a dish or order Chinese food. Instead of spending so much time in the food preparation and house cleaning and table setting, even if you enjoy doing it, alternate with more simple affairs and see what happens!

Travel With Friends and Family

One of the most wonderful things about the women's organization to which we authors belong and where we met is the friends we have made, especially to travel with. In addition to the yearly retreat trips to South or Central America, many of the women travel together throughout the year, from weekend trips to the Berkshires, to sharing houses in Italy, to bidding on trips to each other's houses—where the money goes to a foundation for women and girls. There is something special about the time together with friends and family, exploring new environments, shopping for gifts, riding on a horse, hiking a beautiful trail, cooking together, and laughing about getting lost that gives us stories for the future and strengthens the ties. Take a "guys only" fishing weekend. Plan a girlfriends' weekend to the beach. Friends are family. Family can be friends.

Have One Big Party a Year for Acquaintances

How do you handle the people you enjoy seeing or who have invited you to their home, but you just don't have enough time to be with them? Or whom you like in small doses? Have one big party a year, with fabulous food, lots to drink, and fun things to see or do, and invite them all. It might be a huge barbeque and swim in the summer, a holiday event, a brunch on a winter Sunday, or a dance party with a DJ. Maybe it is to celebrate a special birthday or anniversary, or Super Bowl Sunday. Make it fun. Make it potluck or have it catered, so you can mingle. Spend your time introducing people to each other so they can meet new friends. Enjoy the friends and family you haven't seen for a while. And save time with your spouse or partner or friends to share the gossip afterward!

Pare Down the Holiday Gift and Card List

We all get even busier around the holidays. That added layer of entertaining, gift buying, card writing, decorations, cooking, and travel can have us frazzled. One of the ways we can simplify this fun, but stressful, period is to limit the gift buying and card sending. For example, limit the list of people you give to and tell them ahead of time why. Tell immediate family this year they will get one large gift. Pick names for gifts within the extended family. Give donations to charities in their names. Send a plant or bottle of wine to everyone. Buy gift certificates and cards. Buy throughout the year and label and store the gifts in a closet. Wrap everything in bags with tissue and grosgrain ribbon or with one or two types of gift wrap and the same color bows and ribbon. Order and ship gifts online. Give experiences rather than gifts, such as a frequent flier ticket or a weekend at your beach home or two nights of home-cooked meals delivered to their house.

Instead of sending Christmas or Hanukkah cards, send cards at Thanksgiving. Create a border for an e-mail letter and send it electronically to friends and family. Send postcards rather than cards in an envelope. Use Facebook to stay connected throughout the year.

The idea is to find a way that everything doesn't come due in December. Spread out the tasks that you can so you can enjoy the time with friends and family seeing a movie, going ice skating or to a pueblo dance, baking cookies with a grandchild, or just sitting and reading a great book before a fire with music playing and the snow falling outside.

Use Social Media

The growth of social media has created even more ways we can stay in touch with our family, friends, and colleagues. Facebook allows you to send messages, comment on messages and photos, and reach a large group at the same time. Twitter allows you to send short messages to many. Instagram or Pinterest allow you to share photos and pictures and art. LinkedIn allows you to communicate with colleagues. Use them all to stay connected, but think about the time you spend on social media and how that takes you away from being with friends and family in person or from enjoying so many other things. It is all about balance. Think in terms of minimizing and maximizing use of social media. Where do you get the maximum use of it? By being on Facebook to send news or remember birthdays? How can you minimize use of it?

Facing the Hurdles

Simplifying your life can be a scary thought. *What if I actually had more time to think or plan or do things? Would that mean I would have to do those things I say I really want to do, like take an art course, or visit my cousins in France, or learn Spanish? What if I failed or am too lazy or didn't like doing those things?* We are often our own worst enemies. The same things that keep us from doing what we say we want to do can slip us up on simplifying our lives as well.

Multitasking and Not Enjoying the Moment

Many of us claim to be great multitaskers and it often helps us to handle the many facets of our lives. But multitasking can also be a distractor.

Research shows that when you are multitasking, you are not remembering nearly as much and may often make mistakes. When we are doing more than one thing at once—talking while cooking, texting while in meetings, reading e-mails while on a phone call, or sorting bills while talking to the children—we often are "not in the moment" and not enjoying the simple pleasures of life. Try for just one day not to multitask. Do one thing at a time. Take pleasure in doing the one thing.

Getting Around Feeling Overwhelmed

The first thing that we say after we say we want to simplify our lives is that we are too busy, or it takes too much effort, or it is overwhelming. So how do we get around that feeling of being overwhelmed? The experts say break it up into manageable chunks! Set a timer or time period, say, "I will do whatever I can in 20 minutes or an hour," and stick to it.

You can commit to that time period and then you can come back for another hour another time. Or start with small spaces. The closet or a chest of drawers. Do one each day. Don't try to do everything in one day or weekend, and don't pull everything out and leave it sitting.

One of the other tricks is to break larger tasks down into smaller tasks and do the hardest or most disagreeable or one you keep putting off, first. Start with cleaning out the refrigerator or sanding the rusted iron fence, or putting your finances online. If you do the worst task first—when you have more drive and energy—you will feel a real sense of accomplishment and a lightening of your feelings. You had forgotten how long your head had been reminding you to do that one thing! Now you can go celebrate or congratulate yourself—or dive into a much easier task.

Other ideas for when you are feeling overwhelmed include doing monotonous tasks, which, according to a recent University of California study, boost creativity and problem-solving; volunteering, which triggers the release of feel-good hormones; or sitting down and writing a letter of gratitude, which can improve happiness and rewire the brain's pleasure circuits.

Procrastination as a Habit

We all tend to procrastinate from time to time. Sometimes it is a good thing. We may feel some sort of intuition about doing the task. Or we may have other priorities. We may think the need for the task will go away or someone else will do it if we don't. Or there may be other reasons we ought to pull out and look at. If procrastination is more of a habit for you than an occasional choice, it's best to delve into why it has become so. There usually is a good reason, and by understanding the underlying reluctance, you will not only get past the procrastination, you will have better insights on yourself.

Perfectionism and How to Know When Enough Is Enough

One of the reasons we don't get around to simplifying our lives is our perfectionism. Stemming from our childhood, we either got rewards for trying to be perfect or were punished for not trying. Or we thought we were only loved if we were perfect and did things perfectly. But we aren't perfect, thank goodness. Just think how boring that would be! And we are loved for our imperfections. So knowing when "enough is enough" is a good way to combat those feelings and help us get on with making our lives more simple and joyful. Be yourself. Be authentic. We hear this a lot, and it is an important piece of wisdom. The more we are comfortable with who we are, what we like and dislike, and how we live our lives, the happier and less perfectionistic we will be.

Overcoming Guilt

Sometimes guilt keeps us from simplifying our lives. We don't deserve more time to ourselves, we think, or we fear others will consider us lazy and unmotivated. We feel we should do everything we can and be busy enjoying life, even if it kills us.

> *Stuart was always behind in watching shows on television and began to record more and more programs. But he never had the time to watch them and felt guilty about that. He solved the issue by stopping recording the shows and making a special effort to watch in real time the one or two shows highest on his list.*

What Are Your Fears?

Simplifying our lives is a very important goal, one that all of us should have on our "bucket lists." It makes us more serene. It gives us more time to do what we want. It removes some of the stress. It allows us to feel more in control of what we can control in our lives. So what keeps you from doing it? What are your fears?

Exercise 10-1: Hurdles to Simplifying Your Life

List five areas where you think you need to simplify your life, and list the hurdles to getting you there.

- ❐ Think about why you put hurdles to what you really want to do.

- ❐ Beside each hurdle, write some ideas on what you need to do to get around those hurdles.

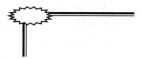

Conclusion

Begin at once to live, and count each separate day as a separate life.

—Seneca

We hope this book has been an inspiration to start planning for your next chapter in life. The "R" word becomes more exciting and less threatening as we see ourselves following our dreams and having the time to reboot and reinvent ourselves. In fact, we feel as though we are starting a revolution—against the old meaning of retirement. Here are some highlights from the book to help you on your way!

* **Planning.** It's critical to your successful transition to the next chapter. It is the basis for all other aspects, and is best done with those who are affected by it.

* **Make your money last** by saving more, investing wisely, keeping your skills and knowledge up to date, working longer, and cutting costs. All more easily done than you thought!

* **Reinvent into new work.** This can not only can keep you relevant and fulfilled, it can enhance your financial situation and lessen your concerns about the future.

* **Find what you can do with your time.** This is one of the most fun parts of your next chapter, from volunteering to tapping into your creativity to renewing old friendships.

* **Don't let Retirement Robbers keep you from really enjoying this next chapter**—whether it is your issues or others demanding your time. Saying "no" gracefully can become an art!

* **Learn how to renegotiate your relationships at home.** This is one of the first skills to develop and is the basis for a happy time with others.

* **Know the tools of a healthy life, and own your own health.** So many people tell us the most important part of enjoying the next chapter is having good health. Do what you can now to prevent problems in the future.

* Most Boomers want to **leave a legacy.** What will be yours? Your reputation? Your philanthropy? Your values? Your business? Your foundation?

* **Simplify your life.** This enables you to follow your passions better. From downsizing to sorting to giving things away, removing the clutter in your mind as well as living space will help you be ready for new things.

You are about to embark on a new journey, one that will be the best in your life. Approach it with enthusiasm and joy. We hope this book will help you along the way and that you will join us with your story at *www. revolutionary-retirement.com* and by participating in our retreats, blogs, tweets, and Facebook posts.

In the meantime, you may want to take the Retirement Readiness Questionnaire After Reading *The Retirement Boom* (available in the Appendix and on our Website) and see where you now are in creating your next chapter and joining the retirement boom!

Best wishes!

Catherine Allen, Nancy Bearg, Rita Foley, and Jaye Smith

Reboot Partners, LLC

APPENDIX

Recommended Resources by Chapter

Chapter 1: The "R" Word: Reboot and Reinvent Rather Than Retire

Retirement Readiness Questionnaire Before Reading *The Retirement Boom*

You may not know all the answers yet, but this exercise will at least get you thinking about your next chapter. Think about your desires before you think about your resources. You can marry the two later. Start here by assessing where you are and a general sense of what you want. Invest some time in it.

*Downloadable version available at:

www.revolutionary-retirement.com/private

Password: Revolutionary

What Is Your Story So Far and What Do You Want?

* What have you loved doing all your life?
* What have you liked about your work over your lifetime so far?
* What haven't you liked?
* How much longer do you want to work at your current job?

* Do you want to continue working either full- or part-time?
* How much longer do you think you need to work to have enough money to retire?
* What do you want to do after you leave your current job? List five things that interest you.
* How do you want to feel in your next chapter of life?
* Are you ready in your heart and mind to retire from your full-time job now, or when do you want to retire?
* Where did you grow up and where do you live now?
* Where do you want to live?
* When does your spouse/partner plan to retire?
* What does your spouse or partner want to do?

Financial and Health Questions

* Are you financially prepared for retirement?
* Do you need to continue to work and bring in money in retirement?
* How is your health?
* Do you have any chronic illnesses that may impact retirement?
* Do you have financial and/or physical responsibility for your parents or older relatives?
* Do you still have financial responsibility for your children or grandchildren?
* Do any other relatives live with you?

Wrap-Up

* What questions do you need to consider to know *when* you want to retire?
* What questions do you need to answer to know *if* you can retire at that time?
* To whom do you need/want to talk about retiring and answering the preceding two questions?

Articles

Pollard, Kelvin, and Paola Scommegna. "Just How Many Baby Boomers Are There?" Population Reference Bureau, April 2014.

Chapter 2: Planning and Designing Your Reinvention

Action Planning Grid

Find a printable version on our Website (*www.revolutionary-retirement.com/private*).

GOALS	ACTION STEPS	WHO CAN HELP	TIME FRAME

Team of Experts Planning Grid

Find a printable version on our Website (*www.revolutionary-retirement.com/private*).

YOUR GOAL	WHAT TEAM EXPERT DO YOU NEED?	WHO CAN HELP

Websites

Technology

geeksquad.com—in-house and online technical and support service

Society6.com—iPhone and tablet cases, and other cool and fun stuff

Apps

Appolicious—for iPhone/iPad users; helps you to identify the right apps for your needs and then to manage them

App Brain—for Android users; helps you to identify the right apps for your needs and then to manage them

Courses/Assistance to Teach You Software and Technology Skills

Apple One to One—if you purchase an Apple product, we recommend you purchase a year of training; $99 for weekly one-on-one training sessions on any Apple product

Genius Bar—for Apple products advice and training at Apple stores

Goldstar.com and *Groupon.com*—for discount deals on courses

SeniorNet (*seniornet.org*)—nonprofit organization that provides adults education, and access to, computer technologies

Technology courses online in how to use Microsoft Office Suite, Word, PowerPoint, Quicken, QuickBooks, Instagram, etc.

ed2go.com

goskills.com

Lynda.com

skillshare.com

Check your local newspaper or college listings for courses or students available to help.

Chapter 3: Making Your Money Last

Go to the following Website links to get the MyMoneyCheck-Up® Questionnaire and the Budgeting and Financial Records worksheets:

* *www.revolutionary-retirement.com/private*
* *sharpentoday.org* or *mymoneycheckup.org/syff* for the Sharpen Your Financial Focus Questionnaire
* *synovus.com* for the Financial Planning Questionnaire

Publications

AARP Bulletin

AARP: The Magazine

Consumer Reports

Kiplinger Retirement Report

Money Advisor

Money Magazine

Websites

Resources

AARP (*aarp.org*)

National Aging in Place Council (*ageinplace.org*)

Employee Benefit Research Institute (*ebri.org*)

Ageing Well Network (*ict-ageingwell.net*)

National Foundation for Credit Counseling (*nfcc.org*)

Osher Lifelong Learning Institute (*olli.gmu.edu*)

National Retirement Planning Coalition (*retireonyourterms.org*)

Financial Management

aarp.org/fraudwatchnetwork

aarp.org/savemoney

bottomlinepublications.com

consumerfinance.gov/complaint

consumerreports.org

fraudavengers.org

aarp.org/money

medicare.gov

mymoney.gov

nfcc.org

cnnmoney.com

reversemortgage.org

sharpentoday.org

socialsecurity.gov

Retirement

aarp.org

aarp.org/retirementcalculator

lifereimagined.org

lifespan-roch.org

retireonyourterms.org

Organizing Finances

bankrate.com/calculators.aspx—personal finance calculators

finance.yahoo.com—links to top finance Websites

naic.org/cis—to check out insurers

quickbooks.com—accounting software

quicken.com—personal financial and money management software

realclearmarkets.com—access to all top money managers and journalists

turboscanapp.com—document scanner on cell phones and other devices

uphelp.org—for help on insurance issues

yacenter.org—young kids bank

www.caregiverslibrary.org/caregivers-resources/grp-checklists-forms. aspx—end-of-life checklists and forms

jazmine.com—a safe way to store all of your personal and financial information

Wealth Management

betterment.com

marketriders.com

personalcapital.com

raymondjames.com

retirement.prudential.com

synovus.com

troweprice.com/ric

wealthfront.com

Budgeting

intuit.com

learnvest.com

mint.com

mollopes.com

yodlee.com

youneedabudget.com

Budgeting Apps

bdgt.me

billguard.com

levelmoney.com

spendeeapp.com

Credit-Related Resources

annualcreditreport.com

cardratings.com

cfpb.gov

consumerdebit.com

creditcards.com

freecreditscore.com

sharpentoday.org

Finding Work

arise.com

encore.org

kellyservices.com

manpower.com

nytimes.com/boss

patinasolutions.com

Volunteering

earthwatch.org

globalvolunteers.com

pivotplanet.com

reserveinc.org

seniorentrepreneurshipworks.org

wsj.com/encore

Travel/Home Trading

airbnb.com

backroads.com

couchsurfing.com

familyadventures.com

homeaway.com

homeexchange.com

onefinestay.com

roadscholar.org

roomorama.com

vrbo.com

wheretoretiremagazine.com

Articles

Brooks, Rodney. "Will You Outlive Your Savings?" *USA Today,* July 16, 2013.

Coombes, Andrea, "For Older Workers, Here Is Where the Jobs Will Be." *Wall Street Journal,* October 2, 2012.

Granger, Amelia. "Men Retire to Mars. Women Retire to Venus." *The Christian Science Monitor,* May 25, 2013.

Greene, Kelly. "Social Security: Wait or Not?" *Wall Street Journal,* January 4, 2014.

Gustke, Constance. "Retirement Plans Thrown Into Disarray by a Divorce." *The New York Times,* June 27, 2014.

Halpert, Julie. "A Way to Keep a Foot in the Corporate Door." *The Wall Street Journal,* January 13, 2014.

Hawthorne, Fran. "When Boomers Inherit, Complications May Follow." *The New York Times,* February 11, 2014.

HealthView Services. "2015 Retirement Health Care Costs Data Report," March 2015. *www.hvsfinancial.com/PublicFiles/Date_ Release.pdf.*

Marchione, Marilynn. "Delayed Retirement Could Prevent Dementia." *The New Mexican,* July 16, 2013.

Prior, Anna "Ten Ways You're Probably Leaving Money on the Table." *Wall Street Journal,* February 10, 2014.

Chapter 4: Reinventing Into New Work

Websites

Career Exploration

aacc.nche.edu

aarp.org

boomerjobs.com

encore.org

escapefromcubiclenation.com

lifereimagined.org

nextavenue.org

pivotplanet.com

retirementjobs.com

seniors4hire.com

whatsnext.com

workforce50.com

Barter

barternationalexchange.com

barterquest.com

bizx.com

imsbarter.com

itex.com

moneycrashers.com

southwestbarterclub.com

swapright.com

swaptreasures.com

trashbank.com

u-exchange.com

Starting Your Own New Business and Self-Employment

BizBuySell (*bizbuysell.com*)

Federal Citizen Information Center (*publications.usa.gov*)

Franchise Zone (*entrepreneur.com/franchises*) (*Entrepreneur Magazine*)

grants.gov—federal government grants

legalzoom.com—preparing legal documents

liquidspace.com—find work or meeting space

moneycrashers.com—market online (*Wall Street Journal*) financial planning

nyc.gov/html/sbs/html/home/home.shtml—small business services, mentoring, small grants

quirky.com—investors looking to see new pitches of business ideas

Resource Associates Corporation (*rac-tqi.com*)

Small Business Administration (*sba.gov*)

startupjournal.com—guidance for small business owners to understand, manage and market online (*Wall Street Journal*) *vistaprint.com*—business cards

zazzle.com—business cards

Virtual Support

elance.com—hire freelancers and find freelance positions

evirtualservices.com—people to support you

odesk.com—remote hires to support you

Smart Source (*smartsource-inc.com*)—technical staffing solutions

Interim Management

Excellence in Management sourcing (*eim.com*)

interimmanagement.com—financial jobs

interimpartners.com—financial jobs

roberthalf.com—financial jobs

wahve.com—insurance industry jobs at home

Angel Investing

angelcapitalassociation.org

goldenseeds.com

indiegogo.com

kiva.org

zidisha.org

CrowdSourcing

(getting funding or ideas from groups of people through online communities)

blurgroup.com

castingwords.com

clickworker.com

crowdspring.com

crowdtap.com

indiegogo.com

istockphoto.com

kickstarter.com

mturk.com

namingforce.com

99designs.com

onforce.com

poptent.com

threadless.com

tongal.com

Board Service

catalyst.org

crenshawassociates.com

directorsandboards.com

nacdonline.org

onboardbootcamps.com

womencorporatedirectors.com

Excellent programs can be found at NACD, Corporate Board Member (NYSE), or Outstanding Directors Exchange (ODX) and at Universities such as Stanford, Harvard, Chicago, Penn, and many more.

Board Profile Questions, Sample Board Interview Questions, and Networking Tips

Find printable versions of these on our Website (*www.revolutionary-retirement.com/private*).

Articles

Bluestone, Barry, and Melnik, Mark, "After the Recovery: Help Needed: The Coming Labor Shortage and How People in Encore Careers Can Help Solve It." Dukakis Center Publications. Paper 7, 2010.

Gandal, Cathy. "Boomers Mean Business." *AARP Bulletin*, March 2011.

Howe, Jeff. "The Rise of Crowdsourcing." *Wired,* June 2006.

Luke, Wayne. "The Right Way to Shift Sectors." *Harvard Business Review* Blog Network, October 1, 2009.

Chapter 5: What Will I Do With My Time?

Websites

Where to Live and Lifestyle

aarp.org—for where to live, travel, and more

thethreetomatoes.com—lifestyle for women Baby Boomers

Meditation

See **Chapter 8: Most Important of All: Your Health** resources.

Reconnection

facebook.com

facetime.com

freeconferencecalling.com

skype.com

tango.me

tumblr.com

instagram.com

Travel Websites

General

eBags.com—for lightweight and durable travel bags of all colors and sizes

aarp.org—travel ideas, trips, and other related information

Discount Travel Brokers

abercrombiekent.com—for luxury trips, and any exploration online of the activities you seek

agoda.com

asiatranspacificjourneys.com—Asia luxury travel

backroads.com—for outdoor adventures

booking.com

expedia.com

hipmunk.com

intrepidtravel.com—800 scheduled itineraries worldwide

kensingtontours.com—rare and remote excursions

lonelyplanet.com—informative travel books

nationalgeographicexpeditions.com—educational trips

nationalparks.org—travel and live for free in U.S National parks

nps.gov—U.S. National Parks

ohranger.com—find parks nearest you

orbitz.com

othgi.com—camaraderie, discounts, and great trips for people 50 and over

priceline.com

roadscholar.org—educational adventures created by Elderhostel

silversea.com—cruises for seniors

travelfish.org—lower-cost South East Asia travel

travelmonkey.com

venere.com

worldnomadstravel.com—lowcost travel

Hotels and Other Advice

hopstop.com—find directions in most major cities

hoteltonight.com—deep discounts on last-minute rooms

iexitapp.com—takes guesswork out of road trip pits stops

mint.com—keep track of your budget while you're traveling, planning the next step, etc.

roadtrippers.com—generates routes, calculates mileage, and estimates gas cost

sitorsquat.com—has user ratings

tripit.com—a mobile app to organize your travel and share itineraries

wimdu.com—hotel reservations

Write Travel Blogs with Photographs

instagram.com

quora.com

tumblr.com

wordpress.com

Resources to Post Pictures or Stories

flickr.com

instagram.com

medium.com

postagram.com—create a customized postcard with your own photo and text and mail it through the app (Postage is 99 cents.)

storybird.com

Learn a Language in Another Country

ef.edu

flsas.com

linguaserviceworldwide.com

Renting/Trading Homes and Apartments

airbnb.com

homeaway.com

homeexchange.com

sabbaticalhomes.com

seniorshomeexchange.com

tripping.com rentvillas.com vrbo.com

Volunteering

aarp.org/giving/back—general advice

American Red Cross (*redcross.org*)

Big Brothers/Big Sisters (*bbbs.org*)

encore.org—general advice/how-to

Environment Alliance for Senior Involvement (*easi.org*)

experiencecorps.org—tutor and mentor

Hospice Foundation (*hospicefoundation.org*)

humanesociety.org—animal shelter volunteer

learningally.org—read for the blind and dyslexic

Make a Wish Foundation (*wish.org*)

Meals on Wheels (*mowaa.org*)

mentoring.org—be a mentor

Peace Corps (*peacecorps.gov*)

proliteracy.org—adult literacy volunteer

score.org—small business mentoring

Volunteer Travel

abroaderview.org

crossculturalsolutions.org

earthwatch.org

enkosiniecoexperience.com

familysabbaticals.com

globeaware.org

gviusa.com

Non-Profit Boards

boardnetusa.org—matches non-profit boards and new leaders

boardsource.org—good governance practices for nonprofit boards, funders, partners

Public Service and Activism

americorps.gov

encore.org

nationalservice.gov

nationalservice.gov/ senior-corps

peacecorps.gov serve.gov score.org

sierraclub.org serve.gov

Photography Schools and Workshops

alisonshaw.com—workshops on Martha's Vineyard

mainemedia.edu—workshops in Maine

santafeworkshops.com—workshops in Santa Fe

tonystromberg.com/workshops—horse workshops in the U.S. and elsewhere

Check local listings for coaches, classes, workshops, and camera clubs.

Writing

capecodwriterscenter.org

thesantafewriters.workshop.com

writers.com

writingclassses.com

writersinstitute.gc.cuny.edu

writersstudio.com

writersworkshop.uiowa.edu

Culinary Programs

amandier.fr—L'Amandier, Provence, France

belcampoinc.com—Belcampo, master classes in chocolate in jungles of Belize

bespoke-beijing.com—Beijing, China

castellodivicarello.eu—Tuscany, Italy

dehouche.com—Virgilio Martinez, Lima, Peru

foxglovefarmbc.ca— British Columbia, Canada

hanoicookingcentre.com—Vietnam

ice.edu—Institute for Culinary Education, New York City

internationalculinarycenter.com—New York, California, Italy

langloisnola.com—New Orleans, Louisiana

los-dos.com—Los Dos Merida, Mexico

naturalgourmetinstitute.com—New York City

philipkuttysfarm.com—Kerala, India

rhodeschoolofcusine.com—Dar Liqama, Marrakech, Morocco

santafeschoolofcooking.com—Santa Fe, New Mexico

schoolofartisanfood.org—Nottingham, England

theagrariankitchen.com—Tasmania, Australia

twobordelais.com—13th-century Chateau La Louviere, France

willingfoot.com—Maine

Other Creative Endeavors

creativityworkshop.com—creativity workshop

creativelive.com—creative classes

Continuous Learning

Ed.Ted.com—educational videos on a wide variety of topics; allows you to upload your own lesson plans

Edx.org—take college courses online from leading universities

KhanAcademy.org—teaches you any type of math; helpful in giving your kids and grandkids help with homework

SkillsShare.com—technical courses

Udemy.com—hundreds of courses in every imaginable category

Chapter 6: Retirement Robbers and Other Challenges

Staying on Track

See the resources for **Chapter 2: Planning and Designing Your Reinvention.**

Websites

Single Life Activities

abercrombiekent.com—for luxury trips

backroads.com—for outdoor adventures

See the resources for **Chapter 5: What Will I Do With My Time?** for many more ideas.

Dating Over 50

aarp.org/dating

eharmony.com

match.com

ourtime.com

seniorfriendfinder.com

seniormatch.com

seniorpeoplemeet.com

Widowerhood

aarp.org—A Guide for the Newly Widowed

Articles

Schwartz, Pepper. "Eight Ways to Find Love Online," *aarp.org,* July 15, 2011.

Chapter 7: Renegotiating Life at Home

Websites

See the resources for **Chapter 5: What Will I Do With My Time?** for resources regarding activities and friends.

See the resources for **Chapter 8: Most Important of All: Your Health** for resources regarding caregiving.

Articles

Singletary, Michelle. "Living With Family When the Money Runs Out." *Washington Post,* May 31, 2013.

Chapter 8: Most Important of All: Your Health

Websites

Health and Wellness

aarp.org

Alcoholics Anonymous (*aa.org*)

al-anon.alateen.org—for families of problem drinkers

American Society of Consulting (*ascp.com/find-senior-care-pharmacist*)—to find a trained pharmacist to consult about your medicines and conditions

The Center for Mind-Body Medicine (*cmbm.org*)

everydayhealth.com—wide range of information

health.gov—health information for individuals and families

International Council of Active Aging (*icaa.cc*)

The Mayo Clinic (*mayoclinic.org*)

thirdage.com—a health Website for Boomers and beyond

Newsletters

belvoir.com/titles/index.html—a list of general and topic-specific newsletters for men and women

Newsletters for Men

menshealthadvisor.com—Cleveland Clinic newsletter for men

mayoclinic.com/health/mens-health/MY00394—Mayo Clinic for men

Newsletters for Women

deniseaustin.com/newsletter—Denise Austin newsletter

health.harvard.edu/newsletters/Harvard_Womens_Health_Watch—Harvard Women's Health Watch

Healthy Action

aarp.org—balance exercises

aarp.org/health/fitness/info-09-2010/tai_chi_chih.html—simpler and gentler version of tai chi (t'ai chi chih)

Exercise Equipment for Home

amazon.com

performancehealth.com

You Tube videos

WalMart, Walgreens, sports stores

Walking, Healthy Diet, and Other Technology Support

amazon.com/health—pedometers in all price ranges

Healthwatch360.com—eating and health-tracker app for iPhones

ihealthlabs.com—iHealth for devices from glucose meters to fitness

myfitnesspal.com/apps—apps to track calories and fitness

new-lifestyles.com—pedometers

rei.com/learn/expert-advice/heart-rate-monitor.html—heart rate monitors

trekdesk.com— a workstation at your desk where you can walk as you work

Brain Health

aarp.brainhq.com—brain training

readersdigest.ca/food/healthy-food/6-foods-help-prevent-alzheimers?id+2—foods to help prevent Alzheimer's

helpguide.org/elder/alzheimers_prevention_slowing_down_treatment.htm—Alzheimer's prevention

lumosity.com—brain games

Meditation and Yoga

calm.com—online or app

dhamma.org—Vipassana Meditation

eomega.org/learning-paths/body-mind-spirit—Omega Center

Headspace app (iOS and Android)—to learn meditation; you can try it for free for 10 days

Kripalu Center for Yoga and Health (*kripalu.org*)

peterrussell.com/HMWET/index.php—"How to Meditate Without Even Trying" online course

susanpiver.com—Open Heart Project offering a weekly talk and e-mails to encourage meditation

umassmed.edu/cfm/about/index.aspx—Jon Kabat-Zinn books and online videos regarding mindfulness. See Center for Mindfulness.

yogaglo.com—yoga classes online; two-week free trial allows you to access their beginner's course on meditation

More Mental and Spiritual Health

aarp.org/health/conditions-treatments/info-03-2011/

creativityandpersonalmastery.com and *areyoureadytosucceed.com*—resources and books to help you think and feel differently and always better and happier

opencenter.org—sound healing at the Open Center in New York

soundstrue.com/shop/Living-in-Gratitude/4395.pdf—living in gratitude

tai-chi-helps-fight-depression.html—tai chi helping with depression

Caregiving

Caregiver Action Network (*caregiveraction.org*)

healthcarechaplaincy.org—spiritual comfort

Healthcare

aarp.org/health/health-insurance/info-06-2012/understanding-long-term-care-insurance.html—"Understanding Long-Term Care Insurance"

fidelity.com/inside-fidelity/individual-investing/fidelity-estimates-couples-retiring-in-2013-will-need-220000-to-pay-medical-expenses-throughout-retirement—study on healthcare costs for retiring couples

freelancersunion.org/benefits—insurance for the independent workforce

healthcare.gov—U.S. government health insurance Website

ltcfeds.com—the federal long-term care insurance program

Medicaid (*medicaid.gov*)

Medicare (*medicare.gov*)

medicare.gov/supplement-other-insurance—supplemental and other insurance for Medicare

Tricare.mil—for retired military personnel under 65

Aging and End-of-Life Planning and Documents/Legal Documents

everplans.com—management and storage of documents online

tn-elderlaw.com/Family_Resources/How_to_Use_a_ Durable_Power_of_ Attorney tn-elderlaw.com/Family_Resources/Links

See Resources for **Chapter 3: Making Your Money Last** for keeping track of documents, accounts, insurance.

Living Will

http://uslwr.com/formslist.shtm—forms for all 50 states and the District of Columbia

Find more information about Living Wills on our Website:

www.revolutionary-retirement.com/private.

Articles

Agnvall, Elizabeth, "How Exercise Affects the Brain and Improves Memory," AARP Blog, July 24, 2015.

Duffy, Jill. "The Best Activity Trackers for Fitness." *PCmag.com,* May 21, 2014.

HealthView Services. "2015 Retirement Health Care Costs Data Report, March 2015. *www.hvsfinancial.com/PublicFiles/Date_Release.pdf.*

Howard, Beth. "Age-Proof Your Brain." *AARP Magazine,* February/March 2012.

Hu, Winnie. "Mom, Dad, This Playground's for You," *New York Times,* June 29, 2012.

James, BD, RS Wilson, LL Barnes, and DA Bennett. "Late-Life Social Activity and Cognitive Decline in Old Age." Rush Alzheimer's Disease Center, Chicago, Illinois 60612. Cited on National Public Radio, April 15, 2013.

Marano, Hara Estroff. "Laughter: The Best Medicine." *Psychology Today,* April 5, 2005.

Melnick, Meredith. "Meditation Health Benefits: What The Practice Does to Your Body." *Huffington Post,* April 30, 2013.

Parker-Pope, Tara. "Suicide Rates Rise Sharply in U.S." *New York Times,* May 2, 2013.

Reynolds, Gretchen. "Getting a Brain Boost Through Exercise." *New York Times,* April 16, 2013.

Tabr, Ferris. "Let's Get Physical: The Psychology of Effective Workout Music." *Scientific American,* March 20, 2013.

Chapter 9: Leaving Your Legacy

Websites

Philanthropy

charitynavigator.com

guidestar.com

foundationsource.com

Scrapbooking, Memoirs, and Journals

apagefromyourlife.com

capecodwriterscenter.com

picasa.com

pinterest.com

shutterfly.com

snapfish.com

Ancestry

23andme.com

ancestry.com

Articles

Brodesser-Akner, Taffy. "The Merchant of Just Be Happy." *New York Times* December 28, 2013.

Hannon, Kerry. "Family Foundations Let Affluent Leave a Legacy." *The New York Times,* February 11, 2014.

Healy, Michelle. "Thanksgiving Talk Could Dish a Helping of Family History." *USA Today,* November 20, 2013.

Smith, Craig. "Guide to Savvy Giving." *The New Mexican,* July 14, 2013.

Svobada, Elizabeth. "Hard-Wired for Giving." *Wall Street Journal,* August 31, 2013.

Thaler, Richard H. "Financial Literacy Beyond the Classroom." *New York Times,* October 6, 2013.

Chapter 10: Simplifying Your Life and Living a Life of Passion

Websites

Places That Will Take Your "Stuff"

Boys and Girls Club of America (*bgca.org*)

Craigslist.org

HabitatforHumanity.org

eBay.com

Kars4Kids.org

Goodwill.org

SalvationArmyusa.org

Trading Homes.

See resources for Chapter 5: What Will I Do With My Time?

homeaway.com

homeexchange.com

vrbo.com

Team of Experts

aarp.org

Certified Financial Planners

ecochi.com—a Feng Shui expert who can help get your home in harmony

elance.com—virtual assistants

Simplifying

bargains.htm

consumerworld.org/pages

containerstore.com

dayataglance.com

familycircle.com

housepad.com

imperthomemaking.com

lifereimagined.com

monster.com

organizedhome.com

realsimple.com

renttherunway.com

simplybeing.com

taskrabbit.com

thefind.com

thetileapp.com

uber.com

zipcar.com

Conclusion

Retirement Readiness Questionnaire After Reading *The Retirement Boom*

*Downloadable version available at

www.revolutionary-retirement.com/private

Password: Revolutionary

We suggest filling out this questionnaire after you have read *The Retirement Boom* and done the exercises. If you can answer these questions, you are well on your way to having a great vision and plan for your next chapter—or for knowing your key unanswered questions. There's no right or wrong. It's about what you want and need, as well as what pace you want.

Vision

❑ Do you have a vision of the lifestyle you want in your next chapter of life?   Yes_____   No_____

❑ What is it? (Describe at some length but then be ready for the next question.)

❐ Can you describe it in a short, positive statement? What is that? (This comes in handy for reminding yourself and for telling other people.)

❐ When do you think you want to begin moving toward this next chapter?

❐ What are key goals and dates?

❐ Will you be moving to another town? Where?

❐ Will you be moving to a different place in your town, such as downsizing?

❐ What is the timing for moving?

❐ Can you take a break to work on envisioning and planning your retirement?

❐ When would that be and how would you do it?

❐ Have you done your Bucket List?

❐ Have you done your Circle Goals?

Financial Facts

❐ Have you met with your personal financial advisor?

❐ Have you met with the financial/benefits advisor at work?

❐ Do you have a financial plan, including consideration of:

   ✴ Expenses for health in later life?

   ✴ An idea of how long you might live? (Many will live 30 years after retirement.)

   ✴ Expenses for your children or parents now or in the future?

   ✴ All income, including Social Security and pension?

   ✴ Assets such as property, extra car, stamp collection.

❐ Do you think you have enough money to carry out your vision?

❐ Will you need to continue to work/earn income?

❐ How can you save more money? List five ways.

❐ How can you reduce expenses? List five ways.

❐ How can you invest in yourself as an asset?

Continuing to Work or Volunteer

☐ If you either need or want to continue to work, what work do you want to do?

   ✳ Is it a passion for you? Does it need to be?

☐ If you want to volunteer, what do you want to do?

   ✳ Is it a passion for you? Does it need to be?

☐ If you are unsure what you want to do, have you done a skills assessment and also asked your colleagues and friends about your strengths?

☐ How will you move to the kind of work/volunteering you envision?

☐ What is the timing?

Other Activities

☐ What do you want to do with your free time? List three main things and two other things.

☐ Do you have a plan?

   ✳ What do you need to do to incorporate at least one of those activities in your life?

Health

☐ How is your health? Is it able to support your going forward into a vital chapter of life?

☐ What do you need to do differently and what can you do?

   ✳ Eating. (Make a list.)

   ✳ Exercise—body. (Make a list.)

   ✳ Exercise—brain. (Make a list.)

   ✳ Fun, companionship, social activities.

☐ Have you filled out key documents for later in life?

   ✳ Will.

   ✳ Living will.

   ✳ Durable power of attorney.

   ✳ Emergency point of contact.

   ✳ Information for children/family members, including your doctors, key documents, and family health history.

❑ Are you caring for a family member?

Legacy

❑ What kind of legacy do you want to leave, remembering that it is a way to make a difference to your family, community, or something larger?

❑ What do you need to do to advance your legacy or legacies?

Simplifying

❑ Do you have ideas about simplifying your life in daily life, work, home, finances, or relationships?

  ✳ Which areas would you simplify and how?

Support

❑ Have you discussed all of this with your:

  ✳ Spouse/partner?

  ✳ Children?

  ✳ Employer?

  ✳ Close friends who give good advice or may be affected?

❑ Are you and your spouse/partner on the same page?

❑ When does your spouse/partner plan to retire?

❑ What does your spouse/partner want to do?

❑ Where do you agree or disagree?

  ✳ How can you resolve differences?

❑ What/who do you need on your Team of Experts, such as help with technology, exercising, financial advice, etc.?

  ✳ Do you have a plan for getting this help?

❑ Will you have Retirement Robbers?

  ✳ Who (including you)?

  ✳ What can you do about it?

  ✳ Do you have an "elevator speech" that will allow you to protect your time and set boundaries?

❑ What challenges could arise at home as you share space in a new way?

* Do you and your spouse and/or other family members have a plan?

Wrap-Up

☐ What questions do you need to answer to know when you want to retire? You can go back and star them on this questionnaire, and also list them here.

☐ To whom do you need/want to talk about retiring and answering the questions above?

Recommended Books

Alboher, Marci. *The Encore Handbook: How to Make a Living and a Difference in the Second Half of Life* (New York: Workman Publishing, 2013).

Allen, Catherine, Nancy Bearg, Rita Foley, and Jaye Smith. *A Journal for Inspiration: Reboot Your Life* (CreateSpace, 2013).

Allen, Catherine, Nancy Bearg, Rita Foley, and Jaye Smith. *Reboot Your Life: Energize Your Career and Life by Taking a Break* (New York: Beaufort Books, 2011).

Arrien, Angeles. *Living in Gratitude: A Journey That Will Change Your Life* (Boulder, Colo.: Sounds True, Inc., 2011).

Berkheimer-Credaire, Betsy. *The Board Game: How Smart Women Become Corporate Directors* (Santa Monica, Calif.: Angel City Press, 2013).

Bolles, Richard, and John E. Nelson. *What Color Is Your Parachute? For Retirement: Planning a Prosperous, Healthy, and Happy Future*, Second Edition (New York: Ten Speed Press, 2010).

Borchard, David, and Patricia A. Donohoe. *The Joy of Retirement: Finding Happiness You've Always Wanted* (New York: Amacom Books, 2008).

Breathnach, Sarah Ban. *Simple Abundance: A Daybook of Comfort and Joy* (New York: Warner Books, 1995).

Bridges, William. *The Way of Transition: Embracing Life's Most Difficult Moments* (Jackson, Tenn.: De Capo Press, 2001).

Bryan, Mark, with Julia Cameron and Catherine Allen. *Artist's Way at Work: Riding the Dragon: Twelve Weeks to Creative Freedom* (New York: William Morrow and Company, Inc., 1998).

Callanan, Maggie, and Patricia Kelley. *Final Gifts: Understanding the Special Awareness, Needs, and Communications of the Dying* (New York: Simon & Schuster, 1992).

Ciriorio, Jeffrey J. *The Complete Idiot's Guide to Retirement Planning* (New York: Alpha Books/Penguin Group, 2007).

Collamer, Nancy. *Second-Act Careers: 50 Ways to Profit From Your Passion During Semi-Retirement* (New York: Random House, 2013).

Crowley, Chris, and Henry S. Lodge, MD. *Younger Next Year Journal: Turn Back Your Biological Clock* (New York: Workman Publishing Company, 2006).

Crowley, Chris, and Henry S. Lodge, MD. *Younger Next Year. Live Strong, Fit and Sexy—Until You're 80 and Beyond* (New York: Workman Publishing Company, 2004).

Crowley, Chris, and Henry S. Lodge, MD. *Younger Next Year for Women. Live Strong, Fit and Sexy—Until You're 80 and Beyond* (New York: Workman Publishing Company, 2004).

Didion, Joan. *The Year of Magical Thinking* (New York: Knopf, 2005).

Duhigg, Charles. *The Power of Habit: Why We Do What We Do in Life and Business* (New York: Random House, 2012).

Duneier, Debra. *EcoChi: Designing the Human Experience* (New York: New Voices Press, 2011).

Freedman, Marc. *Finding Work That Matters in the Second Half of Life* (New York: Public Affairs, 2007).

Freedman, Marc. *Prime Time: How Baby Boomers Will Revolutionize Retirement and Transform America* (New York: Public Affairs, 1999).

Goldberg, Natalie. *Writing Down the Bones: Feeling the Writer Within* (Boston, Mass.: Shambala Books, 2005).

Isaacson, MD, Richard S., and Christopher N. Ochner, PhD. *The Alzheimer's Diet: A Step-by-Step Nutritional Approach for Memory Loss Prevention and Treatment,* Volume 1 (Miami, Flor.: AD Education Consulting, Inc., 2013).

Jason, Julie. *The AARP Retirement Survival Guide: How to Make Smart Financial Decisions in Good Times and Bad* (New York: Sterling Publishing, 2009).

Jones, Landon Y. *Great Expectations: America and the Baby Boom Generation* (New York: Coward, McCann and Geoghegan, 2008).

Kingston, Karen. *Clear Clutter With Feng Shui: Free Yourself From Physical, Emotional and Spiritual Clutter Forever* (New York: Random House, Inc, 1999).

Kotlikoff, Laurence J., and Scott Burns. *The Coming Generational Storm: What You Need to Know About America's Economic Future* (Cambridge, Mass.: The MIT Press, 2004).

Kushner, Harold. *When Bad Things Happen to Good People* (New York: Random House, 1978).

Lamott, Anne. *Bird by Bird: Some Instructions on Writing and Life* (New York: Anchor Books/Doubleday, 1994).

Lee, MD, Roberta. *The SuperStress Solution: 4-Week Diet and Lifestyle Program* (New York: Random House, 2010).

Leider, Richard J., and Alan M. Webber. *Life Reimagined: Discovering Your New Life Possibilities* (San Francisco, Calif.: Berrett-Koehler Publishers, 2013).

Light, Paul C. *Baby Boomers* (New York: W.W. Norton and Company, 1988).

Litchfield, Michael. *In-Laws, Outlaws, and Granny Flats* (Newtown, Conn.: The Taunton Press, 2011).

Marano, Hara Estroff. *A Nation of Wimps: The High Cost of Invasive Parenting* (New York: Broadway Books, 2008).

Niederhaus, Sharon Graham, and John L. Graham. *All in the Family: A Practical Guide to Successful Multigenerational Living* (Plymouth, UK: Taylor Trade Publishing, 2013).

Orman, Suze. *The Nine Steps to Financial Freedom* (New York: Crown Publishers, 1997).

Paull, Candy. *The Art of Simplicity: Living Life by the Essentials of the Heart* (New York: Stewart, Tabori and Chang, 2006).

Pillemer, Carl. *Thirty Lessons for Living: Tried and True Advice From the Wisest Americans* (New York: Penguin Group, 2011).

Ramsey, Dan. *The Everything Start Your Own Consulting Business Book* (Avon, Mass.: Adams Media, 2009).

Russell, Cheryl. *100 Predictions for the Baby Boom: The Next 30 Years* (New York: Plenum Press, 1987).

Ryckman, Pamela. *Stiletto Network: Inside the Women's Power Circles That Are Changing the Face of Business* (New York: Amacom, 2013).

Sandlin, Eileen Figure, and Entrepreneur Press. *Start Your Own Consulting Business* (New York: Entrepreneur Press, 2010).

Savage, Terry. *The Savage Truth on Money* (New York: John Wiley and Sons, Inc., 1999).

Schultz, Patricia. *1,000 Places to See Before You Die,* Second Edition (New York: Workman Publishing Company, Inc., 2011).

Sedlar, Jeri, and Rick Miners. *Don't Retire, REWIRE!* (New York: Alpha Books, 2007).

Servan-Schreiber, David. *Anticancer: A New Way of Life* (New York: Viking, 2009).

Simon, Senator Paul. *Fifty-Two Simple Ways to Make a Difference* (Minneapolis, Minn.: Augsburg Books, 2004).

Sinetar, Marsha. *Do What You Love: The Money Will Follow: Discovering Your Right Livelihood* (New York: Paulist Press, 1987).

St. James, Elaine. *Living the Simple Life: A Guide to Scaling Down and Enjoying More* (New York: Hyperion, 1998).

Stoddard, Alexandria. *Making Choices: Discover the Joy in Living the Life You Want to Lead* (New York: Avon Books, 1994).

Taylor, Paul, and the Pew Research Center. *The Next America* (New York: Public Affairs, 2014).

Trausch, Susan. *Groping Toward Whatever or How I Learned to Retire (Sort Of)* (Hingham, Mass: Free Street Press, 2010).

Yeager, Jeff. *How to Retire the Cheapskate Way* (Three Rivers Press, 2013).

Zelinski, Ernie J. *How to Retire Happy, Wild, and Free: Retirement Wisdom That You Won't Get From Your Financial Advisor* (Anada: Visions International Publishing, 2009).

*All Websites and resources are also available at *www.revolutionary-retirement.com/resources.*

*To access all printable documents, visit *www.revolutionary-retirement.com/private* (password: Revolutionary).

Index

About the Authors

Catherine Allen, Nancy Bearg, Rita Foley, and Jaye Smith, authors of *Reboot Your Life: Energize Your Career and Life by Taking a Break, A Journal for Inspiration: Reboot Your Life,* and *Revolutionary Retirement: What's Next for YOU?* and co-founders of Reboot Partners, LLC, have "walked the talk" in reinventing themselves and redefining their own retirements. They are Boomers themselves, in their 60s, and are four high-energy professional women of diverse backgrounds and successful careers. Their experience ranges from academic to corporate to national security to consulting and teaching, as well as leadership in nonprofits. They have successfully redefined their own lives, having all left major career paths to reboot and reinvent into new chapters.

They met at a conference in 2006 and published their first book in 2011. They offer retreats, workshops, consulting to corporations, and individual coaching, and are active on Facebook, Twitter, Instagram, and LinkedIn. They have appeared on Fox Business News, NBC, and Martha Stewart Radio, and were interviewed in the *Wall Street Journal, New York Times,* and *Bloomberg News,* among many other media.

The co-authors formed Reboot Partners, LLC in 2011 to further their research and work on the topics of sabbaticals, life balance, and retirement planning. They currently are providing consulting and programs targeted at employees and customers of large organizations who are in the pre-retirement or just-retired categories. Over the past two years, they have developed articles, blogs, retreats, targeted corporate programs, and non-profit programs to help Boomers and others plan for the next chapter of their lives.

The inspiration for *The Retirement Boom* came from their own experiences in reinventing their careers, as well as talking to more than 300 people and 30 organizations to gather examples for the book. Rich discussions in the more-than-50 retreats, lectures, and workshops they have held in the last five years added to the issues the book covers.

CATHERINE ALLEN is the financial expert of the group and spent most of her career in the corporate sector at Dun and Bradstreet, at Citicorp, and as CEO of a financial services consortium, BITS, part of the Financial Services Roundtable. She also spent time in academia as a business professor. Today, she is chairman and CEO of The Santa Fe Group and a nationally known expert in cybersecurity, risk management, and emerging technologies. She sits on corporate boards, including Synovus Financial Corporation, El Paso Electric Company, and Houlihan Lokey Investment Bank's Advisory Board, as well as numerous nonprofit boards, including chairing the board of the National Foundation for Credit Counseling and co-chairing the Capital Campaign for the University of Missouri. She served in the past on the Stewart Title Information Services and NBS Technologies corporate boards. She is the co-author of two other books, *The Artist's Way at Work,* with Julia Cameron and Mark Bryan, and *Smart Cards: Seizing Strategic Opportunity,* with William Barr. Catherine has a BS from the University of Missouri, an MS from the University of Maryland, and is ABD from George Washington University. She is active in public policy, and lives with her husband in Santa Fe, New Mexico, and Cape Cod.

NANCY BEARG is a nationally known expert in national security and served in the White House, at the Pentagon, and on Capitol Hill in various high-level positions during a 40-year career in international security policy, including being National Security Advisor to Vice President George H.W. Bush and serving on the National Security Council staff for four years. Earlier, Nancy was the first woman professional staff member on the Senate Armed Services Committee, headed an office in the Office of the Secretary of Defense working on Middle East issues, and was Deputy Assistant Secretary of the Air Force for Manpower and Personnel. She has been an executive, senior advisor, or board member of a number of non-profits, including the Aspen Institute, where she authored five books on national security, conflict prevention, and poverty. She was president and CEO of Enterprise Works Worldwide. In addition to her Reboot Partners work, she is an adjunct professor at the Elliott School of International Affairs at George Washington University, teaching leadership. Nancy holds a BA from Willamette University and a master's of public policy from Harvard University. She resides in Washington, DC.

RITA FOLEY is a retired Fortune 500 Global President with extensive experience building plants, design firms, and successful packaging businesses around the world while being president and SVP at MeadWestvaco Corp. Prior to that, she spent 20 years in the high-tech industry leading substantial growth as EVP of the software company QAD, and at Digital Equipment Corporation, where she worked for 17 years. Today, she sits on the boards of publicly traded PetSmart and Dresser-Rand, and The HealthCare Chaplaincy. Rita also leads the board services practice at Crenshaw Associates. She is a former member of the boards of Pro Mujer International, Council of the Americas, and Wall AG. Rita was honored by NACD for their Inaugural Not-for-Profit Director of the Year Award. Rita is also an accomplished photographer. She held her first solo show in New York City in December 2013. Educated in the United States and abroad, Rita received her diploma from the University of Geneva and a BA with honors in psychology from Smith College, and she graduated from Stanford's Executive MBA Program (SEP). Rita resides in New York City and the Berkshires.

JAYE SMITH is our resident expert on navigating careers, leadership development, and executive coaching. She has spent more than 30 years working with individuals, helping them take charge of their careers and lives. Her company, Breakwater Consulting, formed in 2003, works with Fortune 500 executives to manage and develop their careers, leadership styles, and team effectiveness. Previously Jaye was co-founder and president of Partners in Human Resources International, a full-service consulting firm. She continues to work with them in designing and delivering programs. She worked with JPMorgan Chase's Career Services Program as well as a number of boutique consulting firms before Partners. Jaye is an adjunct faculty member at New York University's Center for Career Planning, as well as at CUNY's School of Professional Studies. She co-authored *Venus Unbound* and has appeared on radio and TV on related career and life balance topics. Jaye co-chairs the board of Harlem Dowling Westside Center. Jaye has an MA from New York University in counseling psychology and a BA in theatre from the City College of New York. Jaye lives in New York City and Sag Harbor, New York.

You can reach the authors through their Website (*www.revolutionary-retirement.com*); on LinkedIn, Facebook, and Twitter; or via e-mail at info@rebootpartnersllc.com.

Also by Catherine Allen, Nancy Bearg, Rita Foley, and Jaye Smith

Reboot Your Life: Energize Your Career and Life by Taking a Break

A Journal for Inspiration: Reboot Your Life

Revolutionary Retirement: What's Next for YOU?

www.revolutionary-retirement.com

Cathy Allen, Nancy Bearg, Rita Foley, and Jaye Smith invite you to visit their Website and continue with your exploration of your next chapter of life. The Website contains articles, important news, videos, worksheets, tips, and interesting links, and it is an invaluable source of relevant information. Updates on what the Reboot Partners are working on, as well as their most recent articles and workshop schedules, are regularly posted.

Photo copyright Hollis Rafkin-Sax
Left to right: Nancy Bearg, Catherine Allen, Rita Foley, Jaye Smith